T0301343

THE PRODUCTION OF EVERYDAY LIFE IN ECO-CONSCIOUS HOUSEHOLDS

Compromise, Conflict, Complicity

Kirstin Munro

BRISTOL
UNIVERSITY
PRESS

First published in Great Britain in 2023 by

Bristol University Press
University of Bristol
1–9 Old Park Hill
Bristol
BS2 8BB
UK
t: +44 (0)117 374 6645
e: bup-info@bristol.ac.uk

Details of international sales and distribution partners are available at bristoluniversitypress.co.uk

British Library Cataloguing in Publication Data
A catalogue record for this book is available from the British Library

ISBN 978-1-5292-1147-4 hardcover
ISBN 978-1-5292-1149-8 ePub
ISBN 978-1-5292-1148-1 ePdf

Cover design: Liam Roberts Design
Front cover image: iStock/jchizhe
Bristol University Press uses environmentally responsible print partners.
Printed by CPI Group (UK) Ltd, Croydon, CR0 4YY

FSC
www.fsc.org
MIX
Paper | Supporting
responsible forestry
FSC® C013604

To Wilson

Contents

Acknowledgments

To keep this section reasonably brief, I would like to limit these acknowledgments to people who directly contributed to the development and publication of this book. First, this book would not be possible without the disproportionate, underrecognized, and undercompensated contingent teaching labor of adjuncts and lecturers at St. John's University in the Department of Economics and the University of Texas Rio Grande Valley in the Department of Political Science. In particular, I would like to thank my UTRGV colleagues Hafthor Erlingsson, Kay Ford, William A. Gordon, James Parisot, Sarah V. Perez, Ruth Ann Ragland, Bryant William Sculos, Andrew H. Smith, Michael Todd Smith, and Robert W. Velez. I am grateful to Nathan DuFord, Rob Hunter, Mary C. King, Maria Kromidas, Loren Lutzenhiser, Gary Mongiovi, Chris O'Kane, Greg Schrock, Jim Strathman, and many anonymous referees for reading all or part of this book and proposal at various stages and providing extremely helpful comments. I am also indebted to Hannah Archambault, Elizabeth Blake, Renate Bridenthal, Zachary Busse, Joshua Clover, Mònica Clua-Losada, Ann E. Davis, Amy De'Ath, Geert Dhondt, Thomas Familia, Sam Fisher, Terence Garrett, Ashley George, Nona Glazer, Donald W. Jones, Adrienne Kahn, Michelle Lamanet, Nate Lavey, Kanyanat Lertkhonsan, Paul Lightcap, Dana Logan, Rob Lucas, Susan Lutzenhiser, Alice and Staughton Lynd, Sam Menefee-Libey, Paul Mishler, Mithra Moezzi, Mary Oak, Luke A. Petach, Luke Pretz, Paddy Quick, Steve Rosen, Pavlos Roufos, Ian Seda-Irizarry, Brendan Seibel, Khalifa Shamoon, William Sokoloff, Zoe Sutherland, Canan Tanir, David Timerman, Aaron Tuller, Lise Vogel, Mason Weiss, Anastasia C. Wilson, and Andrew Woods for conversations that influenced the thinking that is reflected here. Deep gratitude is owed to Catherine Mertes and the late George Tolley, who made the research that forms the basis of this book possible. I am immensely grateful to Paul Stevens at Bristol University Press for seeing potential in me as a book author and for indulging my harebrained ideas, and to everyone at Bristol University Press whose work contributed to the publication of this book. Andrew Ascherl has provided invaluable assistance at various stages of this project, for which I am incredibly grateful. A travel grant from Catholic Relief Services enabled me to attend the Political Ecology Network (POLLEN) biennial conference in 2018 to present an earlier version of Chapter 5; thank you to Meghan J. Clark for coordinating this grant and to the attendees of the POLLEN18 conference for their helpful comments, especially Sarah Bracking, Madeline Davis, and Anne Meneley. I would like to thank Betsy Kauffman for inviting me to share my initial results with her colleagues at the Energy Trust of Oregon in the summer of 2017. Tom Bunyard graciously invited me to present this research at the University of Brighton's Centre for Applied Philosophy, Politics, and Ethics in 2019, where I received helpful comments from the audience; thanks are due to Tom Bunyard, Lara Perry, Eric John Russell, and one anonymous member of the audience who has extremely incorrect ideas about porridge cooking times. I am grateful to the Critical Political Economy Research Network of the European Sociological Association for inviting me to speak at their workshop in 2021 about the theoretical model in Chapter 2, with special thanks owed to Jule Goikoetxea and David Bailey. I am bound by the terms of a longstanding but highly dubious legal agreement to thank the 1978 LP *Cheap Trick Live at Budokan*. I am grateful to *Science & Society* and Guilford Press for allowing me to reproduce in this book sections of my 2019 *Science & Society* article, "Social Reproduction Theory, Social Reproduction, and Household Production." I am grateful to SAGE Publications for permission to reproduce in this book sections of my 2018 article in *The Review of Radical Political Economics*, "Unwaged Work and the Production of Sustainability in Eco-Conscious Households," and my 2021 article in *Environment and Planning E*, "Solid Waste Management and their Meanings in Ecologically Conscious Households." To all of my friends and fellow creatures: thank you! Finally, and most importantly, I would like to thank my informants for sharing their time and the intimate details of their everyday lives with me.

Introduction:
"This Can't Be All Up to Me"

On the grid

Partway through my interview with Heather—a nurse, doula, lactation consultant, multilevel marketing essential oils saleswoman, and White mother of three young children—she excused herself for a moment to check on the placenta that she was processing in an electric fruit dehydrator. Dehydrating, grinding up, and then encapsulating placentas into pill form for easier postpartum ingestion is just one of Heather's many side hustles related to natural living. By this point in my interviews with ecologically conscious parents in and around Portland, Oregon, in the Northwestern United States, I had learned to maintain a neutral demeanor when confronted with unusual practices and comments that made me feel uncomfortable or with which I disagreed. But the essential oil diffuser gently misting the air in Heather's immaculately clean home took on a different meaning knowing that a human placenta was cooking in the next room. I felt immediately queasy, but I did my best to act like this was the most normal thing in the world. Great, no problem. I channeled the neutral "brisk nurse" affect I was taught to use as an interviewer for a lesbian health study years earlier but had mostly refrained from using in this study in favor of the warmer affect I hoped would generate good rapport with my eco-conscious informants. As soon as I got back into my car after the interview, I pulled out my phone and googled: "is eating placenta cannibalism?"

Heather told me, "My husband tells me that I can't do it all, and I understand that, but we can make little steps and those will all be helpful. Anything we can make and be away from consumerism and capitalism." In contrast to her own difficult childhood, Heather has deliberately arranged her life to devote as much time as possible to her children, and she works hard to protect her children from harm. She has been breastfeeding continuously for the past seven years, nursing each of her older children until they were at least four years old. During our interview, she was breastfeeding and bargaining with her youngest child—a two-year-old—to please eat her lunch instead of nursing more. Heather researches health choices for her family extensively, and she is very skeptical of conventional medicine and cleaning products, both of which she generally avoids. When it comes to her interest in sustainability and natural health and parenting, Heather believes that balance is key. She doesn't want to live what she calls an "Into the Wild" off-the-grid lifestyle with children who are constantly naked and covered in mud. Heather prefers to integrate natural living into a more moderate, contemporary way of life.

Heather said to me very earnestly, "It was so easy to have you over because this is something that I'm so passionate about. It's our life." I think her sentiment captures the reason that 37 parents of young children were willing to take time out of their busy schedules to speak with me for an hour or two about how they get things done in everyday life. These parents are doing their best to bring their hectic everyday lives into alignment with their pro-environmental values and concerns while still remaining "on the grid," and I left nearly every interview feeling deep admiration and respect for my informants. However, as my discomfort with Heather's dehydrating placenta might imply, the purpose of this book is not to promote these activities and interventions—even if that is what my informants thought or hoped I would be doing as I studied the production of everyday life in their households.

Background

Over the past half-century, environmental problems involving atmospheric emissions, resource depletion, toxic releases, and ecosystem degradation have become increasingly serious and seemingly intractable (Brown 2003; Rosa & Dietz 2003). The sources of these problems are often attributed to large global social forces such as capitalism (Schnaiberg & Gould 1994; Foster 2002), industrialization (Malm 2015), or affluence (Ehrlich & Ehrlich 1974; Dietz & Rosa 1997). Attribution has focused on particular industries, such as fossil fuel extraction and refining, electric utilities, internal combustion transportation, and mechanized agriculture. But these systems and their associated environmental harms exist only by virtue of the fact that they are involved in the production of goods and services destined for consumption by persons and social groups, regardless of the mode of production involved in their transformation and distribution. So, a careless, clueless, or contemptuous consumer is also increasingly portrayed as the root cause of environmental decline on a hitherto unimaginable scale (Jorgenson 2003; Wilk 2016).

In the United States, recent national policy has included initiatives urging citizens to "do their part" and take personal responsibility for the environment and climate change mitigation (The White House 2015; U.S. Environmental Protection Agency 2016; NASA 2017). With the presidency recently held by a man who claimed global warming is a conspiracy "created by and for the Chinese in order to make U.S. manufacturing non-competitive" (Trump 2012) and a Supreme Court decision that curbs the Environmental Protection Agency's ability to limit emissions (Liptak 2022), local governments and environmentally minded people are finding it more important than ever to take environmental protection into their own hands (Bondar 2017; Bromley-Trujillo 2017; Gannon 2017). Families are worried about their health and safety in the face of a federal government that is seemingly unconcerned with their well-being (Levin 2017).

Studies of the "end users" of energy, water, food, and other products are not well developed (Stern et al 1997; OECD 2008). Except for the areas of recycling and energy conservation, public policies and interventions aimed at reining in expectations and demands or changing lifestyles have been fairly rare since they are not compatible with the overarching U.S. celebration of growth and affluence. Energy conservation is an exception because of periodic crises and the clear economic advantage of doing more with less energy. But even in the energy-efficiency movement, there has been reluctance to touch the "third rail" of lifestyle change (Lutzenhiser & Gossard 2000), and well-funded interventions in the most innovative geographies like California have closely adhered to a model that encourages modest energy savings from "cost-effective" technology upgrades (Lutzenhiser et al 2009).

Some research on "green consumerism" has been undertaken, but most often from a marketing or advertising perspective, with aims related to identifying and selling products to consumers with environmental interests. Usually these types of studies include little reference, beyond individual psychology and descriptive demographics, to social science theories or scholarly empirical literatures (Diamantopoulosa et al 2003; Rex & Baumann 2007; Nath et al 2013; Chekimaa et al 2016).

Where studies of consumption have taken place, they often draw upon narrow data sources and surveys that collect limited information about attitudes and actions across large populations. Drawing upon work by Shove et al (1998) and Wilhite et al (2001), Lutzenhiser (2002, 345) considered the prospects of "greening the economy from the bottom-up" and identifies a number of difficulties faced by households with the strongest environmental attitudes and the best intentions, including family dynamics, lack of resources, social pressures, and institutional constraints. Little work has been done to examine those dynamics and factors, or to empirically apply theories that might shed light on them.

If households and their demands for goods and services are even partially implicated in ecological decline, it is important that the dynamics of demand be better understood. However, this is easier said than done. Knight (1944,

3

289) notes that "The treatment of demand is the branch of economic theory in which methodological problems are most important and most difficult. This is because it is here that behavior facts are most inseparably bound up with motivation and that objective data call most imperatively for interpretation by subjective facts and meanings." While there is appropriate social science theory, it is scattered across disciplines and seems to be incomplete in some cases and contradictory in others.

Household production and sustainability

If changes at the household level are desirable for environmental protection, then the need for better knowledge is obvious. For example, it would be important to understand the differences in the understandings, practices, and impacts of "high-demand," "average," and "low-demand" households, as well as differences in practices and beliefs of different socioeconomic demographic groups. Shove (2003, 10) notes that, "In real life, escalators do not run backward. Neither do the escalators of demand in economic theory" in research that outlines the expectations, infrastructures, and social meanings that alter social practices over time in ways that increase the demand for resources. But what does it look like when demand *does* decline?

Because little of this work has been done, and the focus of a book must be manageably narrow, I have chosen to investigate the lives and habits of a group of self-described sustainable households with young children, focusing on the intentional actions the members of these households take to reduce environmental harm. What these households do, why they do these things, how they think about them, and how they evaluate the results all shed important light on how environmental concern can be translated into pro-environmental action under the best circumstances. So, from these households, perhaps we can learn what changes might be possible, what the limits are to their effectiveness, what the unintended consequences of widely promoting these household-level pro-environmental practices might be, and, ultimately, if household-level efforts to mitigate environmental problems are effective or even desirable.

Lutzenhiser (2002, 4) found that "pro-conservation attitudes rarely resulted in action." In response to this challenge, I recruited a sample of action-oriented households who have made fairly major changes to conventional ways of getting things done in everyday life to bring their practices into alignment with their sustainability values. The households I spoke with over the course of this research are not green anarcho-primitivists living off the land in a yurt, raising unwashed feral children, and making their own clothes out of roadkill squirrel pelts—and no disrespect is meant to such households. I have known and cared for many people who live this way. This book just isn't about them. Rather, I deliberately sought out a set of very much on-the-grid households in a metropolitan area living in ways that remain fully engaged with civilization and modernity. Furthermore, I have focused on a portion of the lifecycle when the time and finances of households are under particularly heavy strains, concentrating on adults with young children.

Shove (2003, 9) writes that "studies of eco-villagers or investigations into the beliefs of self-confessed environmentalists represent something of a distraction. What counts is the big, and in some cases global, swing of ordinary, routinized and taken-for-granted practice." The households I spoke with over the course of this research have thought carefully about these routinized practices, and have made changes to their expectations, demands, and how they think about needs in ways that still allow them to remain connected to contemporary society. These households provide a reasonable window into an alternate reality where demand escalators really do run backwards.

Sixteen years in Portlandia

I moved to Portland, Oregon, in the Northwestern United States in the spring of 2001 on a Greyhound bus with everything I owned. A few months prior, I had mailed a "room wanted" flyer I'd made at a copy shop to a few health food stores and schools in the area for their community bulletin boards. My future roommates sent me a Polaroid picture of the house in the mail, and I sent back a money order for my $200 monthly rent, crossing my fingers that it would work. It did work, and before too long I was wearing holes in my secondhand shoes exploring my new city and riding a rickety clunker of a vintage bicycle around town. I marveled at how great it was to live in a place that made it so easy to do the kinds of things I wanted to do—living without a car, eating great vegan food, showering infrequently, and participating in a vibrant radical DIY community of punks and activists. Here, the interests and practices that raised eyebrows in the suburb where I grew up were actually encouraged and celebrated. I moved away a couple times over the years, but Portland kept drawing me back, even as the city became an increasingly expensive caricature of itself, parodied in the 2011–2018 sketch comedy show *Portlandia*—a Disney World playground for professional progressive environmentally concerned adults. Portland is the "greenest city in America," and the whitest one, too. Portland is *Stuff White People Like*, and I had been quietly observing the city and its residents for 16 years—on and off—by the time I began conducting the interviews with eco-conscious parents of young children that form the basis of this book in the spring of 2017.

My personal connection to many of the ideas and practices presented in this book go back to my childhood. Like so many children of the 1980s, I was terrified of acid rain and "the greenhouse effect" that I learned about in science class when I was six, and I was angry that adults weren't doing more to protect the environment. In school, we sang songs about recycling and not wasting food, we kissed banana slugs, and were taught by environmental educators to say, "Thank you, plant!" whenever we picked a flower. I wrote letters to President George H. W. Bush demanding that he protect the pandas, and I picketed my elementary school alone when I was eight years old over a proposal to build a stadium on the habitat of endangered burrowing owls. I listened to bird sounds cassettes in my Walkman instead of New Kids on the Block, and I was banned from bringing pH test strips to my elementary school, where I had been trying to test the water fountains for evidence of acid rain. Even as a young child, I refused to eat at McDonalds out of my concerns for rainforest beef and Styrofoam, dabbled in vegetarianism, and became a vegan at 15. During a severe drought in California, I was taught by my parents not to flush the toilet after urinating, and I shared bathwater with my siblings. My mother, a first-generation Czech immigrant, did not generally put clothes in the tumble dryer, a rarity among our neighbors even in a sunny mild climate. She tried to limit our sugar intake, and, if I begged enough, would occasionally buy me Rainforest Crisp breakfast cereal (produced by Bob Weir and Mickey Hart of the Grateful Dead). I read the book *50 Simple Things Kids Can Do to Save the Earth* and tried to implement as many of the suggested changes as I could. Like my informant Eric, seeing images of wounded animals choking on litter inspired me to cut up six-pack rings into what Eric described poignantly as "the smallest pieces in the world."

Today, I share many practices that my informants might consider "eco-conscious"—for example, I exclusively line-dry my laundry, my household is mostly vegetarian, I avoid the bottled water that is ubiquitous where I live, I have deliberately reduced my air travel, I'm a selective flusher, and I keep my home relatively cold in the winter and hot in the summer. I love to pick up free stuff off the side of the road. I have picked through the recycling in my own household and workplaces to correct others' recycling errors. I was vegan for around a decade, and I bike commuted year-round for many years, including through several freezing Chicago winters. In the past, I regularly took discarded food and other items out of store dumpsters, and I occasionally stole organic food from chain grocery store self-checkouts. One year, I tried to buy nothing from a store with more than one location. Today, I do not see these activities as morally good or my lifestyle as "environmentally friendly." At this point, I participate in many of these purportedly pro-environmental practices without even thinking about it. There are many pro-environmental practices that I know are pointless, counterproductive, or likely not worth the time and effort, but they have become deeply engrained habits over the years.

The critical perspective that I bring to thinking about these practices also goes back decades. During the course of this research, I've returned frequently to memories of living as a teenager in a large Southeast Portland vegetarian eco-cooperative house with my friend and bandmate Mason Weiss and five older environmental hippy types. My roommates did things for work like organizing permaculture events and building mud and hay structures in less-gentrified parts of town to encourage community dialogue and gathering. Two punk teenagers in a house of older hippies sounds like a perfect fish-out-of-water sitcom plot, and it is true—our band may have played a raucous mocking cover of the charity single "We Are the World" at an important permaculture and "placemaking" event we'd been invited to by a roommate. My tenure in the house ended a bit dramatically after we very rudely drowned out a folk music session happening in the living room with our own semi-screamed rendition of "Kumbaya." The culture clash of the house also inspired thoughtful conversations between Mason and I about the potential hypocrisy and limits to the efficacy of pro-environmental practices that inform my thinking and have stuck with me to this day. Our roommates were sweet, well-meaning people and we shared many of their values and goals, but, upon closer inspection, we found their worldviews to be deeply misguided.

At the same time as the hippies-versus-punks culture clash was brewing in my home, another clash that informs this book was developing—I was immersed in studying neoclassical economics, my undergraduate major at an elite liberal arts college. I wore penny loafers and a moth-eaten little boy's tweed blazer I'd found at a thrift store, and I carried around a briefcase that I'd found in a dumpster as some sort of very, very inside joke. When my band was playing a rent money fundraiser at a friend's house, an attendee caught a glimpse of a magazine inside my dumpstered briefcase that I'd left near the door and exclaimed, "Who the fuck is reading *The Economist* here?" Indeed! Who brought *The Economist* to the punk show? I have received a fair amount of negative feedback for my insistence on critically adapting the theory of household production from arch-neoliberal/neoclassical economist Gary Becker (1981) to a Marxist-feminist analysis (see Chapter 2 of this book for the full model). I agree that these theories may seem incompatible and the use of Becker (1981) completely heretical, but I am a contradictory person living in a contradictory and insane world.

Methodological overview

In this book, I am not the main character, but I am present as the narrator whose perspective and subjective interpretations undoubtedly influence the story that is being told. A major difference between my informants and myself is that I have no children and do not ever expect to have any. While I was conducting the interviews for this book, I participated in some afterschool pickups and babysat young children from an eco-conscious family. I wanted to do my best to understand the personal worlds of my informants. Ultimately, this research was generated in collaboration with my informants, and the presentation here embodies the "coproduction of ethnographic knowledge, created and represented in the only way it can be, within an interactive Self/Other dialogue" (Tedlock 1991, 82).

If the household can be thought of as a small factory that produces everyday life, then the research I conducted is a factory visit in the tradition of Smith (2003 [1776]) and Marshall (1919) or a worker's inquiry in the tradition of Marx (Marx 1938 [1880]). I spoke with informants from 23 households living in the Portland–Vancouver–Hillsboro metro area in 60- to 90-minute ethnographic interviews about their everyday lives. During these conversations, I asked my informants to explain how their sustainability priorities influence their practices—or how they get things done—with respect to household waste, comfort, cleanliness, food, transportation, and childcare. My informants get everyday tasks done just like everyone else—by focusing on the things that are most important to them, making use of the resources available to them, and subject to the constraints that limit their options. Their sustainability priorities mean that the practices and precise combinations of inputs involved in the production of their everyday lives are different from conventional U.S. households. This led me to examine the consequences, intended and unintended, of these sustainability-oriented ways of getting things done.

Spradley (1979) argues that the ethnographer achieves this goal of collaborative research by being taught by their research subjects, not by collecting data on them. To learn from my informants, I first had to attempt to assume a "conscious attitude of almost complete ignorance" (Spradley 1979, 4) of the world of pro-environmental practices and sustainability-oriented families. I frequently encountered confused and disturbed looks from the people I was interviewing when I asked them questions like, "Why do you recycle?" I followed up these questions by asking the informants to pretend that I'm from outer space and that I want them to explain normal, seemingly obvious things to me. It wasn't that I was some kind of monster who didn't share their fundamental concern for the environment, a conclusion they might draw about someone who is opposed to recycling or doesn't understand its appeal,[1] but that I wanted to understand their perspective in their own words. I asked my informants to suspend disbelief and to assume I didn't know anything.

While ethnography and field research can frequently mean sustained periods of participant observation lasting months or even years, the ethnographic interview is a method that allows the researcher to make inferences based on what informants say about their beliefs, practices, and artifacts during a shorter study period. Ethnographic interviews are a useful way to study sustainability practices and their meanings in households because "notions of materialism, belief, perception, and values are at the core of the sustainability vision" (Murphy & McDonagh 2016, xiv). The semi-structured ethnographic interview allowed my informants to teach me the meanings of their practices and to guide me to understand what they deem to be important in the environmental realm, without demanding too much of their limited time.

Intimacy, friendship, and feminist research

Some feminist researchers, such as Stacey (1988, 22), suggest that ethnography is particularly well suited to feminist research because the qualities that make for good ethnography—"empathy, connection, and concern"—are also "women's special strengths." However, I am both a woman and a highly experienced quantitative researcher, so I hardly believe that quantitative, positivist approaches to research are inherently male, masculine, or oppressive, and qualitative research methods are inherently female, feminine, and anti-oppressive. Additionally, I reject the notions that women are by nature more nurturing and intuitive or that women possess a natural inclination toward empathy, care, and human connection (Rich 1986, 42).

That being said, over the course of our conversations it was impossible to avoid caring about many of the people who were sharing so much about their everyday lives with me. There is an intimacy involved in sitting in people's homes in conversation, seeing how they live, meeting their children, and holding their babies. I was deeply disturbed by one informant who shared concerns that are linked to notions of "White replacement"—mentioning what he views as the erasure of "European Christian values" due to multiculturalism and low birthrates among White Americans and Europeans—but this interview stands out as uniquely alarming and disquieting. The remaining interviews were pleasant conversations with lovely people who I genuinely grew to like over the brief time we spent together. My informants weren't paid for their time, though I did bring each household a box of organic herbal tea that I purchased at a local food co-op—this is the kind of hostess gift that I would bring to any friend or acquaintance who invited me into their home. Following the interview, each household for whom I had a mailing address received a handwritten thank-you card in the mail, also a personal habit of mine.

The research here is based on respondent-driven open-ended ethnographic interviews, generally volunteered for on the basis of a belief that the informant's views are important and they are contributing to a cause they believe in—sustainability, whatever that term means to the informant. But part of this willingness to share information with me was based on an assumption by many of my informants that I was "one of them" and was producing a piece of research-advocacy that would champion their lifestyles and practices. Stacey (1988) suggests that the intimacy and friendships forged during feminist ethnographic research leaves participants vulnerable to exploitation by the researcher. In this sense, I was indeed exploiting the desire of many of my informants to have their views and practices validated and promoted. As a critical social researcher, however, I did not approach this project from a sustainability advocacy perspective but rather with the goals of critical fact-finding and theory-building in mind.

This is not to say that there are no political motivations underlying this research—this is research *on* sustainability-oriented households and the everyday lives of the people who comprise them, but it is research *for* households and people, too (Stanley & Wise 1990, 21). Like Marshall and Marx, my ultimate concern is with the conditions of people's lives and how those lives and conditions might be improved to promote human flourishing. To these concerns I add a contemporary one—avoiding environmental devastation. While I was humbled and encouraged by major interventions in everyday life that my informants were making in order to bring their practices in line with their values, I remain highly skeptical of the efficacy of individual-level changes in the face of environmental crises. In fact, after listening to my informants' struggles to balance everyday tasks with frequently costly and time-consuming sustainability practices, I emerged from this research even more convinced that the household is the incorrect site for these pro-environmental interventions. This may not be the conclusion some of my informants hoped I would draw from our conversations, but I think they would agree that we are hoping for the same things—healthy people and a healthy planet.

A note on deception

Researchers trained in positivist approaches may also be concerned about the risk of deception in ethnographic interviews. In general, I found all of the informants and their responses to be believable. They tended to be very frank about their everyday lives, including their struggles and frustrations with maintaining habits consistent with their environmental values. They were reassured of their anonymity in the study, frequently believed they were contributing to something important, and would gain little from deceiving me.

Mina: Honestly? [laughs] I don't have any reason to lie to you!

Spouses occasionally disagreed over their partners' portrayal of their habits and motivations, but generally came to some kind of agreement.

Dayna: We've always been pretty conventional on the laundry detergent. And I'm the one who buys the laundry

10

detergent—I don't know if David has *ever* bought laundry
detergent before. But I'm the one that generally buys that.

David: We've gotten the Seventh Generation [brand of natural
cleaning products] and the Bio-Kleen stuff before, but
generally we get Tide or All.

Dayna: We actually *don't* normally get Tide, we only started getting
Tide when we started using cloth diapers.

In this case, Dayna asserted herself as the expert on laundry soap, David
balked, and Dayna reasserted herself and "won" the dispute.

In several interviews, I was able to visually observe that the home's thermostat
was set to a heating temperature higher than the temperature my informants
reported. For example, walking into Scott and Sarah's home on a chilly April
day, I passed the thermostat on my way to their living room and saw it was
set to 72 degrees (Fahrenheit, or 22.2 degrees Celsius). All of the members
of the household, including the children, were wearing short-sleeved tops.
However, they reported their winter thermostat setting to me as 70 degrees
(Fahrenheit, or 21.1 degrees Celsius) during the interview. It could be that
Scott and Sarah were purposefully deceiving me, but based on their demeanor
I do not believe that any deception was deliberate. Perhaps 70 degrees is the
temperature they've programmed their thermostat to, and they increase the
temperature manually when they feel too cold. Or perhaps they were telling me
a temperature they thought was a correct or ecologically righteous one—the
temperature they believe is the maximum ethical heating setting.

A different possible explanation also emerged in a subsequent interview
with two households whose thermostat I didn't observe directly—some
ecologically oriented households alter their typical home heating and cooling
temperatures to accommodate guests.

Penny: I usually keep the heat around 64 [degrees Fahrenheit, or 17.8
degrees Celsius] when I'm home and awake. But my mom
was just here visiting, and she was very cold with 64 so we
had it at 67 [degrees Fahrenheit, or 19.4 degrees Celsius].

Quinn: The thermostat is normally set at 67 or 68 [degrees Fahrenheit, or
19.4 or 20 degrees Celsius] for the environment and also money.
But if guests are over I'll put it up to 70 [degrees Fahrenheit,
or 21.1 degrees Celsius] so that people are comfortable.

However, if my informants were indeed giving misleading answers about
their winter thermostat settings, that too provides important information
about social norms and the values of my informants (Rubin & Rubin 2012,
66–67). It is possible that some of the practices and habits described by the
informants may not be the way they live their lives 100 percent of the time,

but their descriptions may represent the way they believe they ought to be living their lives or what they believe to be norms for people who share their values. In any case, this is valuable information.

Recruiting my informants

The sampling frame for this study was adults in households in the greater Portland–Vancouver–Hillsboro metro area in the Northwestern United States with children under age ten who consider their lifestyles eco-conscious or sustainable. My choice to include only families with children under ten was not an arbitrary one—this allowed me to see how households balance sustainability and other priorities at a point in the lifecycle where resources like time and money are particularly constrained. The Portland metro area is a convenient place to conduct this research, since it is where I was living at the time of the fieldwork, but it is also an ideal place to recruit highly eco-conscious households. The proportion of adults who report being worried about climate change in Multnomah County ranks in the highest 0.01 percent among U.S. counties (Yale Program on Climate Change Communication 2015) at 66 percent. Portland residents routinely rank among the "greenest" in the United States thanks to high rates of non-car transport, renewable energy, and recycling (Svoboda et al 2008; Rogers 2011; Bernardo 2016). This is a useful setting for investigating the practices and the cultural knowledge (symbols, categories, competence, and language) of households who see themselves as particularly sustainable or eco-friendly.

While there are well-documented damaging effects of the ideologies of family and motherhood in capitalism, this is not to say that the benefits, affective or otherwise, that people perceive to flow out of families or the parental role are illusory—rather, "like every proper ideology, the family too was more than a mere lie" (Frankfurt Institute for Social Research 1972, 138). The informants I spoke with for this research love their children and value their families—in fact, for many of my informants, their children and families are the primary motivation for their sustainability practices. However, I have chosen to talk about households rather than families for several reasons. The nuclear family household is a modern concept that has been held up politically as an ideal form (Barrett 1980, 199–213; Munro 2021). The arrangement of biologically related people into shared dwellings in a "family-household"—the combination of "kinship and co-residence"—is a relatively modern social arrangement (Barrett 1980, 199–213) that is not universal across time or cultures (Netting et al 1984). Indeed, the two-parent heterosexual nuclear family household is not universal in the sample of households I interviewed for this research, as several of my informants live with unrelated persons as roommates, in multigenerational households, in cohousing, or in intentional community (see Table 3.1 for a full list of household configurations). While 13 of the households I spoke with for this research live together in a nuclear family with two parents in a heterosexual relationship, the remaining ten do not. They include single fathers, single mothers, multigenerational and multifamily households, a couple in a lesbian relationship, and transgender/gender nonbinary parents.

To recruit my final sample of 23 households, I began by sending an email with a brief description of the study, an image of my recruitment flyer, and a link to a screener questionnaire website to over 150 local professional and personal contacts, asking them to forward my request for participants to people they knew who might qualify. While none of my own contacts or acquaintances participated in the study, several of my informants were one or two steps removed from people I know. I also posted the announcement on the social networks LinkedIn and Switchboard. Informants outside my own social and professional networks were recruited through the online social platforms Facebook and Meetup.org, where I posted recruitment information in large groups for environmentally minded parents, corresponded directly with group organizers, and learned about events. I attended several Meetup. org events for ecologically minded and LGBTQ parents to distribute flyers and tell attendees about my study. The illustration for the flyer was created by my friend Michelle Lamanet, an artist and sustainability-minded parent of two children.

The interviews

As I conducted the interviews that form the basis of this book, it seemed like everyone around me was still reeling from the new and shocking reality of the Donald Trump presidency—protesting the election, protesting the inauguration, protesting the so-called Muslim Ban, counterprotesting against increasingly emboldened far-right White supremacist groups, and supporting jailed antifascist protesters. It was a difficult spring in Portland. A so-called alt-right march for "free speech" came within a few blocks of my home. This march was attended by a White supremacist who went on to murder two men a month later when they intervened to stop him from spewing hate speech at young women on the train, one of whom was wearing a headscarf and one of whom was Black (Wilson 2017). One of the men murdered for intervening to stop the violent White supremacist was Taliesin Myrddin Namkai-Meche, a fellow alumnus of Reed College who had also majored in economics. Namkai-Meche was murdered on the same train that I regularly took to work and school. These murders immediately brought to mind the long history of White supremacist violence in the Pacific Northwest that I learned about as a teenager from my conversations with older Portland punks and SHARPs (Skinheads Against Racial Prejudice), including the 1988 murder of Ethiopian student Mulugeta Seraw by Portland

White supremacists affiliated with the hate groups East Side White Pride and White Aryan Resistance (Langer 2004).

It was all hitting very close to home—both literally and figuratively—and I was experiencing massive regret and self-doubt about my decision to study something so small—the mundane habits and everyday lives of eco-conscious households with children—when it seemed like the country was descending into fascism. I was energized by gathering in the streets and airport corridors with thousands of strangers in protest. The feelings of solidarity as we collectively expressed our shared outrage and fear helped me get through this challenging time. During this same period of frequent protests, I was being welcomed into the homes of strangers who were willing to take time out of their busy day to share with me intimate details about their everyday lives as they attempted—in small and large ways—to promote human and environmental flourishing in a world that is hostile to both. Looking back on this time following two and a half years of extreme isolation as a vulnerable population member during the COVID pandemic, the human connection and intimacy of these interviews in the homes of strangers is almost unimaginable.

During the months of April and May of 2017, I conducted 22 interviews lasting at least 60 minutes each with 37 informants representing 23 households. I interviewed Heather and Gloria, representing two different households, during a single 90-minute joint interview at Heather's home while Gloria and her children were visiting for a playdate. My conversation with Yvonne took place over the phone while her youngest child was napping, since between recent travel and her various obligations it was difficult to find a good time to meet in person to talk. I met with Nathan and Nicole at a busy suburban brew pub in an outdoor mall, I met Leonda at a coffee shop in a strip mall in the suburbs, and I met Wendy at a coffee shop in Southeast Portland. The remaining households invited me to their homes for our interviews. I changed the names of all my informants, with a different letter assigned to each household in roughly the order in which I interviewed them. I only assigned names to informants I interviewed; in households where I spoke with only one member of a couple for scheduling reasons, I did not assign a name to the household members who were not interviewed.

The interviews were open-ended and lasted between 60 and 90 minutes, though I tried to keep our conversations as close to 60 minutes as possible. While I let my informants lead me to the topics they found the most important and interesting, I asked them a set of questions about how they get things done in everyday life in various household realms (waste, comfort, cleanliness, food, transportation, and general provisioning). I asked my informants follow-up questions to help me understand how they developed their current practices, what resources are employed in the production of

14

these practices, what these practices mean to my informants, what their motivations for these practices are, and what they might do differently if they had more time or money. I rarely asked the questions in the exact order of the interview guide, preferring instead for the conversation to flow as naturally as possible.

Outline of the book

In this book, I will introduce you to a group of sustainability-oriented households with young children living in and near Portland, Oregon, in the Northwestern United States. I will describe how they balance their priorities and get things done in everyday life using the resources they have available to them, limited by the factors that constrain them. I will discuss how these households make choices, how these choices have evolved over time, and how they view the social and cultural meanings of these choices.

While I had initially expected to find mostly White nuclear families with relatively high incomes engaging in sustainability practices varying along a green spectrum, my sample of households told a different story. I found that sustainability is not exclusively the domain of the White and affluent. Low-income households typically substituted time-consuming sustainability practices for more costly ones, and they tended to live in ways that involved a lower overall environmental impact than many of their higher-income counterparts in my sample. Low-income households I spoke with lived in smaller dwellings, owned fewer or no cars, and generally consumed less overall—in part out of financial necessity and in part for environmental reasons. The popular conception of a sustainable household might be an affluent White nuclear family installing solar panels on their single-family home and picking up organic meat in their new hybrid vehicle from an overpriced natural foods store. Is my informant Fiona—a single mother who works part-time at a daycare and lives in a small rental apartment with no car, no space-cooling equipment, and no central heating; who goes shopping for vegetarian groceries on the bus and obtains most of what her household needs either free or purchased secondhand—more or less environmentally conscious than an affluent family with a Prius and solar panels? Perhaps it is easier to be "sustainable" when you don't have money to buy many things in the first place.

Clear themes emerged as I was conducting my interviews in the spring of 2017. My informants were exhausted, frustrated, experiencing conflict in their relationships related to their sustainability practices, and often feeling genuinely hopeless about the efficacy of their pro-environmental interventions into mundane daily practices. In the words of my informant Emily: "I can't have this on my shoulders. This can't be all up to me. I'm just going to do the best that I can." They described feeling like the world they live in—even in a "green" city like Portland, Oregon—was not always designed to promote the well-being of their families or the environment. It was based on these interviews and the experiences of my informants that I developed the Marxist-feminist theoretical framework that is presented in Chapter 2. This orienting perspective helped me move beyond description, to adequately make sense of the data, and to identify possible paths forward— as well as which roads to a better world within capitalism may be blocked.

While this theoretical framework was helpful for understanding my interviews, a large portion of my objective in this book is simply to describe things about the everyday lives of eco-conscious households that haven't previously been described in this way in the social science literature, focusing on mundane practices as the unit of analysis. In Chapter 3, I will introduce you to my informants and their households in more detail—I describe who my informants are, who they live with, and their varied priorities in the sustainability realm and motivations for sustainability practices. In Chapter 4, I provide a description of the resources my informants have available to them to get things done, and a description of the factors that constrain them. In Chapters 5 and 6, I investigate specific facets of daily life and describe how these households get things done in ways that are informed by their sustainability priorities using the resources available to them and subject to the factors that constrain them. In Chapter 5, I discuss the disposal of household waste, including trash, recycling, composting, diapers, and toilet waste. In Chapter 6, I describe household practices with respect to indoor comfort temperatures, and household and bodily cleanliness. In Chapter 7, I discuss the role of "doing your own research" and acquiring know-how in the practices and lives of eco-conscious households with young children. Chapter 8 describes the conflicts that arise as a result of priorities and pro-environmental interventions in mundane practices that put my informants out of step with the mainstream. In Chapter 9, I discuss the sometimes painful trade-offs that are required to balance priorities, resources, and constraints in the everyday lives of my informants. I conclude by explaining why households are making these interventions in conventional ways of getting things done and what this might mean for policymakers and others who are considering promoting household-level pro-environmental practices.

Conclusion

Netting et al (1984, xxi) note that "Perhaps it is this mundane, repetitive, cross-culturally obvious appearance of households that has led observers to think of them as unproblematic and lacking in interest." However, Engels (1902, 71) writes that the household represents a microcosm of all of society—within individual households the same conflicts and processes take place as do in the economy and society as a whole. Fractal-like, the household is a miniature economy within the larger economy, a miniature society within the larger society, existing within but subsumed by these larger structures and bound by their laws. Similarly, Marshall (1919) argued that the processes underlying production in the economy as a whole can be understood by examining a single factory, and that production in a single factory can be understood by first examining the economy as a whole. I will argue that this study of sustainability-oriented households and their activities reveals crucial information about society, the economy, and the state. It is these larger structures and institutions that constrain the range of possible actions of individuals and groups. But revealingly, my informants feel obligated to undertake pro-environmental tasks that are often time-consuming and costly because they can't trust institutions to take the large-scale protective actions that they believe are needed for the environment and the health of their families. Even when these household-scale actions are revealed to be futile—or outright counterproductive—my informants continue to press on out of the conviction that their sustainability values and priorities are worthy of their efforts.

In her landmark study of household production, Reid (1934, v) points out that household production is an integral component of the economy, and unless we recognize it as such we will be unable to properly evaluate the costs and benefits associated with moving production into or out of the household. By modeling "green" households as producers of everyday life rather than consumers of environmental products, I bring into focus the additional unwaged work that eco-conscious households undertake to bring their mundane daily practices into alignment with their ecological values. In doing so, we can begin to evaluate the trade-offs inherent in these pro-environmental activities and whether or not the household is a desirable site for pro-environmental interventions.

References

Barrett, Michèle (1980) *Women's Oppression Today: Problems in Marxist Feminist Analysis*, London: Verso.

Becker, Gary S. (1981) *A Treatise on the Family*, Cambridge, MA: Harvard University Press.

Bernardo, Richie (2016) "2016's Greenest Cities in America," *WalletHub*, October 12, Available: https://web.archive.org/web/20161030090939/https://wallethub.com/edu/most-least-green-cities/16246/ [Accessed March 26, 2017].

Bondar, Paul (2017) "A New Era of U.S. Climate Action," *Rocky Mountain Institute Outlet*, June 6, Available: https://www.rmi.org/news/new-era-u-s-climate-action [Accessed June 7, 2017].

Bromley-Trujillo, Rebecca (2017) "Despite Trump, Many Cities and States are Fighting Climate Change: Including Pittsburgh," *The Washington Post*, June 6, Available: https://www.washingtonpost.com/news/monkey-cage/wp/2017/06/06/despite-trump-pittsburghs-working-on-slowing-climate-change-so-are-many-other-cities-and-states/ [Accessed June 7, 2017].

Brown, Lester (2003) *Rescuing a Planet under Stress and a Civilization in Trouble*, New York: W.W. Norton & Company.

Chekima, Brahim, Syed Azizi Wafa, Syed Khalid Wafa, Oswald Aisat Igaua, Sohaib Chekimab, and Stephen Laison Sondoh Jr (2016) "Examining green consumerism motivational drivers: Does premium price and demographics matter to green purchasing?" *Journal of Cleaner Production*, 112: 3436–3450.

Diamantopoulosa, Adamantios, Bodo Schlegelmilch, Rudolf Sinkovicsd, and Greg Bohlenc (2003) "Can socio-demographics still play a role in profiling green consumers? A review of the evidence and an empirical investigation," *Journal of Business Research*, 56: 465–480.

Dietz, Thomas and Eugene A. Rosa (1997) "The effects of population and affluence on CO_2 emissions," *Proceedings of the National Academy of Sciences of the United States of America*, 94(1): 175–179.

Ehrlich, Paul R. and Anne H. Ehrlich (1974) *The End of Affluence: A Blueprint for your Future*, New York: Ballantine Books.

Engels, Friedrich (1902) *The Origin of the Family, Private Property and the State*, translated by Ernest Untermann, Chicago: Charles H. Kerr & Company.

Frankfurt Institute for Social Research (1972) *Aspects of Sociology*, Boston, MA: Beacon Press.

Foster, John Bellamy (2002) *Ecology against Capitalism*, New York: Monthly Review Press.

Gannon, Liz Purchia (2017) "How to Push Climate Action Forward in the Trump Era," *Grist*, March 6, Available: http://grist.org/opinion/how-to-push-climate-action-forward-in-the-trump-era/ [Accessed June 7, 2017].

Jorgenson, Andrew K. (2003) "Consumption and environmental degradation: A cross-national analysis of the ecological footprint," *Social Problems*, 50(3): 374–394.

Knight, Frank H. (1944) "Realism and relevance in the theory of demand," *Journal of Political Economy*, 54(4): 289–318.

Langer, Elinor (2004) *A Hundred Little Hitlers: The Death of a Black Man, the Trial of a White Racist, and the Rise of the Neo-Nazi Movement in America*, New York: Macmillan.

Levin, Sam (2017) " 'Like a Slow Death': Families Fear Pesticide Poisoning after Trump Reverses Ban," *The Guardian*, April 17, Available: https://www.theguardian.com/us-news/2017/apr/17/california-pesticides-central-valley-trump [Accessed June 7, 2017].

Liptak, Adam (2022) "Supreme Court Limits E.P.A.'s Ability to Restrict Power Plant Emissions," *The New York Times*, June 30, Available: https://www.nytimes.com/live/2022/06/30/us/supreme-court-epa/epa-carbon-emissions-scotus?smid=url-share [Accessed August 24, 2022].

Lutzenhiser, Loren (2002) "Greening the economy from the bottom up? Lessons in consumption from the energy case," in Nicole Biggard (ed) *Readings in Economic Sociology*, Oxford: Blackwell, pp 345–356.

Lutzenhiser, Loren and Marcia Hill Gossard (2000) "Lifestyle, status, and energy consumption," *Proceedings of the 2000 ACEEE Summer Study of Energy Efficiency in Buildings*, 8: 207–222.

Lutzenhiser, Loren, Laura Cesafsky, Heather Chappells, Marcia Gossard, Dulane Moran, Jane Peters, Mersiha Spahic, Paul Stern, Elizabeth Simmons, and Harold Wilhite (2009) *Behavioral Assumptions Underlying California Residential Sector Energy Efficiency Programs*, Report to the California Public Utilities Commission, Berkeley: California Institute for Energy and Environment.

Malm, Andreas (2015) *Fossil Capital: The Rise of Steam Power and the Roots of Global Warming*, New York: Verso Books.

Marshall, Alfred (1919) *Industry and Trade: A Study of Industrial Technique and Business Organization; and of their Influences on the Conditions of Various Classes and Nations*, London: Macmillan.

Marx, Karl (1938 [1880]) "A worker's inquiry," *New International*, 4(12): 379–381, Available: https://www.marxists.org/history/etol/newspape/ni/vol04/no12/marx.htm [Accessed August 24, 2022].

Munro, Kirstin (2021) "The welfare state and the bourgeois family-household," *Science & Society*, 85(2): 199–206.

Murphy, Fiona and Pierre McDonagh (2016) "Introduction," in Fiona Murphy and Pierre McDonagh (eds) *Envisioning Sustainabilities: Towards an Anthropology of Sustainability*, Newcastle upon Tyne: Cambridge Scholars Publishing, pp xiii–xxix.

NASA (National Aeronautics and Space Administration) (2017) "NASA's Climate Kids: What Can We Do to Help?" Available: https://climatekids.nasa.gov/how-to-help/ [Accessed June 7, 2017].

Nath, Vishnu, Rupesh Kumar, Rajat Agrawal, Aditya Gautam, and Vinay Sharma (2013) "Consumer adoption of green products: Modeling the enablers," *Global Business Review*, 14: 453–470.

Netting, Robert, Richard R. Wilk, and Eric J. Arnould (1984) "Introduction," in Robert Netting, Richard R. Wilk, and Eric J. Arnould (eds) *Households: Comparative and Historical Studies of the Domestic Group*, Berkeley: University of California Press, pp xiii–xxxviii.

OECD (Organisation for Economic Development and Co-operation) (2008) *Household Behaviour and the Environment: Reviewing the Evidence*, Paris: Organisation for Economic Development and Co-operation.

O'Kane, Chris and Kirstin Munro (2022). "Marxian economics and the Critique of Political Economy," in Werner Bonefeld and Chris O'Kane, eds. *Adorno and Marx: Negative Dialectics and the Critique of Political Economy*. London: Bloomsbury, pp 77–95.

Reid, Margaret (1934) *The Economics of Household Production*, New York: John Wiley & Sons.

Rex, Emma and Henrikke Baumann (2007) "Beyond ecolabels: What green marketing can learn from conventional marketing," *Journal of Cleaner Production*, 15: 567–576.

Rich, Adrienne (1986) *Of Woman Born: Motherhood as Experience and Institution*, New York: W.W. Norton & Company.

Rogers, Stephanie (2011) "Hard Economic Times Be Damned: 10 U.S. Cities Make their Own Green," *Ecosalon*, October 26, Available: http://ecosalon.com/americas-greenest-cities-319/ [Accessed March 26, 2017].

Rosa, Eugene A. and Thomas Dietz (2003) "Footprints on the earth: The environmental consequences of modernity," *American Sociological Review*, 68(2): 279–300.

Rubin, Herbert J. and Irene S. Rubin (2012) *Qualitative Interviewing: The Art of Hearing Data* (2nd edn), Thousand Oaks, CA: SAGE.

Schnaiberg, Allan and Kenneth Alan Gould (1994) *Environment and Society: The Enduring Conflict*, Caldwell, NJ: Blackburn Press.

Shove, Elizabeth (2003) *Comfort, Cleanliness, and Convenience: The Social Organization of Normality*, Oxford: Berg.

Shove, Elizabeth, Loren Lutzenhiser, Simon Guy, Bruce Hackett, and Harold Wilhite (1998) "Energy and social systems," in Steve Rayner and Elizabeth Malon (eds) *Human Choice and Climate Change*, Columbus, OH: Battelle Press, pp 291–325.

Smith, Adam (2003 [1776]) *An Inquiry into the Nature and Causes of the Wealth of Nations*, New York: Bantam Classic.

Spradley, James P. (1979) *The Ethnographic Interview*, Long Grove, IL: Waveland Press.

Stacey, Judith (1988) "Can there be a feminist ethnography?" *Women's Studies International Forum*, 11(1): 21–27.

Stanley, Liz and Sue Wise (1990) "Method, methodology and epistemology in feminist research processes," in Liz Stanley (ed) *Feminist Praxis: Research, Theory and Epistemology in Feminist Sociology*, London: Routledge, pp 20–60.

Stern, Paul C., Thomas Dietz, Vernon W. Ruttan, Robert H. Socolow, and James Sweeney (eds) (1997) *Environmentally Significant Consumption: Research Directions*, Washington, DC: National Academy Press.

Svoboda, Elizabeth, Eric Mika and Saba Berhie (2008) "America's Top 50 Green Cities," *Popular Science*, February 8, Available: http://www.popsci.com/environment/article/2008-02/americas-50-greenest-cities?page=1 [Accessed March 26, 2017].

Tedlock, Barbara (1991) "From participant observation to the observation of participation: The emergence of narrative ethnography," *Journal of Anthropological Research*, 47(1): 69–94.

The White House (2015) "Presidential Proclamation—America Recycles Day, 2015," November 13, Available: https://obamawhitehouse.archives. gov/the-press-office/2015/11/13/presidential-proclamation-america-recycles-day-2015 [Accessed June 7, 2017].

Trump, Donald (2012) "The Concept of Global Warming Was Created By and For the Chinese in Order To Make U.S. Manufacturing Non-Competitive," therealdonaldtrump,11:15 am, November 6, Available: https://twitter. com/realdonaldtrump/status/265895292191248385?lang=en [Accessed June 7, 2017].

U.S. Environmental Protection Agency (2016) "What You Can Do about Climate Change," Available: https://19january2017snapshot.epa.gov/climatechange/what-you-can-do-about-climate-change_.html [Accessed June 7, 2017].

Wilhite, Harold, Elizabeth Shove, Loren Lutzenhiser, and Willett Kempton (2001) "The legacy of twenty years of energy demand management: We know more about individual behavior but next to nothing about demand," in Jochem Ebarhard, Jayant Sathaye, and Daniel Bouille (eds) *Society, Behaviour and Climate Change Mitigation*, Dordrecht, The Netherlands: Kluwer Academic Publishers.

Wilk, Richard (2016) "Consuming ourselves to death: The anthropology of consumer culture and climate change," in Susan A. Crate and Mark Nuttall (eds) *Anthropology and Climate Change: From Encounters to Actions*, London: Routledge.

Wilson, Jason (2017) "Portland Knife Attack: Tension High as 'Free Speech Rally' Set for Weekend," *The Guardian*, Monday, May 29, Available: https:// www.theguardian.com/us-news/2017/may/28/portland-knife-attack-free-speech-rally--sunday [Accessed August 29, 2022].

Yale Program on Climate Change Communication (2014) "Yale Climate Opinion Maps Data—U.S. 2015," Available: https://climatecommunicat ion.yale.edu/visualizations-data/ycom/ [Accessed November 18, 2016].

2

Eco-Conscious Household Production and Capitalist Society

In this chapter, I will present a version of the Marxist-feminist theoretical framework that I originally outlined in my 2019 article in the journal *Science & Society*. This chapter is admittedly dry and somewhat out of step with the rest of the book. If you are less theoretically oriented and more interested in the description of mundane practices I promised you in the Introduction, you can feel free to skip this chapter without missing too much. However, for theoretically oriented readers interested in the debates in Marxist-feminism or household production, this chapter is for you.

I initially developed this model based on what I learned from my eco-conscious informants during the ethnographic interviews I conducted in the spring of 2017. While it is somewhat a cliché that parents of young children are tired, I was nonetheless struck by just how exhausted my informants were. Even the most affluent among them, who had substantial extended family and/or paid assistance with everyday household tasks, were struggling to cope. And even the low-income single mothers in my sample told me that they most needed more time rather than more money. I realized that these households were making substitutions of time for money in producing a version of everyday life that felt more in line with their environmental values. Not only that, but they were taking on additional time-consuming tasks, such as recycling sorting, in order to avoid or "undo" environmental damage from other sites, scales, and sectors. At the same time, my informants were generally deeply dissatisfied with what they perceived to be the overall ineffectiveness of these interventions—no matter how many time-consuming changes they made to their everyday practices, it felt like a drop in the bucket. The environment is still being destroyed, and many of my informants were acutely aware of their complicit role in this destruction despite their best efforts.

Having been trained somewhat paradoxically in both Marxist-feminist and neoclassical theories of household production in graduate school, I was able to draw on these seemingly contradictory frameworks to help me explain what I uncovered in my interviews. As I will explain, other existing theoretical frameworks would point to more reformist or redistribution-oriented solutions to the problems and concerns of my informants. My own somewhat heretical framework suggests that social democratic or progressive solutions are not enough (for reasons described in more detail in O'Kane & Munro 2022). While these social democratic or reformist policies might change the relative extent to which a household relies on time, or money, or state inputs to get things done in everyday life, I conclude, following Collins (1990, 17), that the underlying household production process—to say nothing of capitalist society and its environmental impacts—is left unchanged.

This book is a study of economic and social practices, with household activities that meet the needs of household members seen as *production* rather than *consumption*. I characterize these efforts related to household production as forms of work—whether that work is waged or unwaged. But this waged and unwaged work is not voluntary, but rather is compelled as a consequence of the historically specific organization of capitalist society. Household consumption of goods and services for use by household members is more accurately described as *derived demand* (Mosak 1938)—demand for goods and services that are transformed and used in the production of something else. In this case, that "something else" is everyday life: things like physical comfort, cleanliness, waste removal, adherence to social norms, and, of course, the production and reproduction of the commodity labor-power. Often unwittingly, household members engaged in these quotidian activities contribute to the reproduction of capitalist society as a whole—and the social misery and environmental destruction associated with it. It is this emphasis on the *complicity* of households in the reproduction of capitalist society as a whole rather than the distribution of tasks and credit that is the key difference between my perspective and that of both liberal/progressive feminist economics' examination of "care work" and the recent Marxist-feminist offshoot calling itself "Social Reproduction Theory."

In the theory proposed here, the household and its production processes are implicated in the reproduction of capitalist society. The state, capitalist firms, and households are inextricably linked to one another via their own processes of production and reproduction, with these processes shaped by the imperative of endless accumulation. Ultimately, the household in capitalism is forced to rely on capitalist firms and the state to ensure the survival of its members both day to day and intergenerationally, and in turn the household contributes to the perpetuation of capitalist society. Following work by Vogel (1983), Glazer (1984, 1993), Giménez (1990, 2018), and Collins (1990) on the relationship between unwaged work and capitalist society, it is the interdependencies between households, capitalist firms, and the state in these production processes that lead to the reproduction of capitalist society as a whole. My model of household production critically adapts the theory of household production from neoclassical economics (Reid 1934; Becker 1981) to a Marxist–feminist analysis.

It may seem quite strange to draw on a neoclassical theory of the household that has been so widely criticized in the feminist literature. The key insight I take from Becker (1981) via the emphasis of Carmel and Barry Chiswick (Chiswick 1999; Chiswick & Chiswick 2000) is that varying proportions of inputs can be relied on by the household in its production process as substitutes and complements. Households produce everyday life by making use of the resources available to them and subject to the factors that constrain them. The household can substitute the inputs of unwaged work, commodities purchased with money from waged work, and state inputs in its household production process—producing goods and services for use by household members using the resources available to household members. Returning to Marxist–feminism, redistribution of surplus leading to changes in the proportions of inputs into the household production process do not change the underlying production process, let alone the organization of capitalist society—these changes merely alter the intensity with which the household uses one input or another (Collins 1990, 17).

This systematic model of how production in capitalism is carried out by households, capitalist firms, and the state shows that it is necessary to tie the household and household production to the dynamics of production and reproduction in capitalist society. While the lines between them are blurred, capitalist firms, the state, and households in capitalism are each historically specific configurations of people and production that emerged in their current form as part of the process of the historical development of capitalism. The main inference drawn from this model is that it is not possible to disentangle the everyday life of household members from the reproduction of capitalist society as a whole. Redistribution of wealth and power from the capitalist class to the working class does little to change the underlying production processes that constitute capitalist society as a whole, just the proportion of inputs relied upon in those processes. This points to a different set of strategies and paths forward for the promotion of human and environmental well-being—showing that it is necessary to abolish the organization of production and reproduction that constitutes capitalist society, including the state and household, not merely to reassign the benefits and costs.

Other possible theoretical frameworks

It may seem as if progressive/liberal feminist economics,[1] or the recent Marxist-feminist offshoot Social Reproduction Theory,[2] would be natural theoretical sources to draw on for understanding household production and everyday life in highly ecologically conscious households. In fact, I had fully anticipated, prior to embarking on my fieldwork, to use some version of these theories to explain what I expected to find. However, my informants and the results of my interviews did not line up with my expectations and instead pointed me in a different direction entirely. While there are important political and theoretical differences between progressive/liberal feminist economics and Social Reproduction Theory, they nonetheless share several assumptions that make these theories inappropriate for understanding the results of this study.

These theories emphasize the gendered distribution of waged and unwaged work (in feminist economics) and productive and unproductive labor (in Social Reproduction Theory) between men and women, and the gendered differences in compensation and recognition for that work. However, my informants told me that the gendered distribution of work and the assignment of money, credit, or recognition for that work were not important to understanding their households.[3] As a result, I've emphasized the dynamics and substitutability of inputs into the household production process, and how that same process contributes to the continued existence of capitalism (a bad thing) and thus to the environmental problems that my informants are worried about. No one interviewed for this research described the distribution of work in their households as unfair, nor did they see this work—whether waged or unwaged, productive or unproductive— as particularly virtuous or in need of recognition. Rather, many of my informants see their everyday lives as contributing to environmental problems despite their best efforts.

My informants guided my theorizing here—it was my informants themselves who showed me that waged and unwaged work were interchangeable substitutes in their households. So once again, as the major focus of progressive/liberal feminist economics is the gendered distribution of work and money between men and women, this is an inappropriate framework for this study. Furthermore, a large proportion of my informants do not live in nuclear family households with two parents in a heterosexual relationship, and those who do tell me that the gendered distribution of waged and unwaged work is not a major concern, nor is fairness, nor is the assignment of credit for tasks related to household production. They tell me that unwaged work is important in their households and they see the distribution of work among household members as fair. Thus, while a progressive/liberal feminist economic framework for thinking about household production and its relationship to the economy and society as a whole has many merits, it is not the correct framework for understanding the specific concerns my informants pointed me toward.

Another key difference between the theory that I developed based on my interviews with informants for this study and that of progressive/liberal feminist economics and Social Reproduction Theory is in our understanding of capitalist society and the role of work in that society. Both of these theories examine capitalism from the standpoint of labor, while my model of household production in capitalism encompasses a critique of capitalist society in terms of the organization of production and reproduction (see also Munro 2019; O'Kane & Munro 2022). Whereas both progressive/ liberal feminist economics and Social Reproduction Theory attempt to paint the labor involved in production and reproduction as virtuous, I extend Marx's insight that to be a productive worker is "not a piece of luck, but a misfortune" (Marx 1976 [1867], 644) to argue that the same misfortune is also true for reproductive workers. The basis for my argument here is the view that exploitation and domination are inherent to the organization and processes of production and reproduction in capitalism, and thus that the reproduction of capitalist society proceeds by perpetuating these forms of organization, no matter the rates of exploitation or the amounts of redistribution. Household production in capitalism is not "care" or virtuous "life-making" that takes place outside of capitalism—in fact, households and household production are complicit in perpetuating the capitalist organization of society. After all, "the reproduction of labour-power ... [is] a factor in the reproduction of capital itself. Accumulation of capital is therefore multiplication of the proletariat" (Marx 1976 [1867], 763–764).

This model can be distinguished from these other strains of feminist scholarship that seek to theorize women's oppression while celebrating and valorizing tasks related to household production. Instead, labor in capitalism—whether waged or unwaged, productive or unproductive— should not be viewed as the virtuous and morally enriching source of all wealth, but rather as a key input into the reproduction of capitalist society and its attendant social misery and environmental destruction.

Thus, the matter at hand is not the correct assignment of "credit" for production and social reproduction and the design of redistributive policies on that basis—although such scholarship has added much to our understanding of inequality and the importance of women's work to the economy as a whole. Rather, the theoretical orientation employed here points to the interrelated and overlapping ways capitalism organizes production and reproduction in our everyday lives (Glazer 1993, 38). Glazer points out that when we conceptualize all socially useful tasks as "work" or "labor" we evacuate these concepts of their theoretical power in political economy. There is a troubling productivist tendency on the part of some feminist scholars to define all socially useful activities as "work," with the implicit assumption that "work" is somehow honorable and superior to "nonwork" (Glaser 1993, 37; see also Weeks 2011). For this reason, I use the term "work" throughout this book to specifically point to the role of these activities in household production or commodity production—not to ennoble these activities. If the reproduction of capitalist society is incumbent on the perpetuation of household production, capitalist production, and the state, activities which are valorized by progressive/liberal feminist economists and Social Reproduction Theorists as forms of "work" are integral to this negative process.

The theoretical framework for this book
The reproduction of capitalist society

The underlying understanding of household production employed here is situated in terms of a larger critique of labor and production in capitalism. The reproduction of capitalist society as a whole—that is, social reproduction—can't be examined without an understanding of the contribution of the reproduction of labor-power and the reproduction of capital to social reproduction. Indeed, the political economic concepts of labor-power and the reproduction of capital are meaningless if divorced from their explicit roles in the perpetuation of capitalist society as a whole and from their recursive relationship to each other in the reproduction of capitalist social relations of production.

What makes capitalism different from other modes of production is not exchange in markets, but rather "a system of production in which the production of things is subordinated to the production, appropriation, and accumulation of surplus value" (Clarke 1994, 281). Capitalist society is defined here as not just a capitalist division of labor within the so-called "formal economy" but divisions of labor that compel and constrain the activities of people within society as a whole. These divisions of labor are a consequence of the specific organization of society's productive capacities in capitalism, in which the imperatives of capitalist accumulation ultimately shape institutions and dictate the activities of people. Within the larger social division of labor in capitalist society there are further divisions of labor within each sector that comprises it. Households must purchase commodities using money from waged work and combine these commodities with their unwaged labor in order to survive, and they are thus reliant on firms for both these wages and the commodities purchased with these wages. Firms must purchase labor-power, must drive down costs to earn profits from the sale of commodities, and must constantly reinvest these profits to avoid being put out of business by other firms. The state provides services designed to reduce the welfare losses attributable to the conflict between households and firms, and between actors within each sector; it also provides public goods and infrastructures. Each sector is compelled by the larger structure to act in particular ways to ensure its own survival, and in doing so perpetuates the existence of the whole.

This can be elucidated through a simple model of capitalist society comprised of three sectors, each of which must reproduce itself to perpetuate the existence of the sector: households, capitalist firms, and the capitalist state. This follows the convention in classical political economy, starting with Quesnay and ending with Marx's critique of classical political economy, in which the capitalist economy is conceived of as a system with interconnected parts. What I mean by "sector" is a site of production made up of individual instances that use a production process unique to that sector. The production process of each sector is dictated by the imperatives of accumulation. This imperative arose out of the historical process of primitive accumulation that divided people and production into these sectors and separated producers from the means of production. It is this imperative of accumulation as a law of the whole—rather than one sector or another or one class or another—that ultimately prescribes and constrains the possible actions taken by people, firms, and institutions. Each sector must use inputs from other sectors in their production process to produce outputs that are in turn used by other sectors. These sectors are not "separate spheres," but rather should be seen as interdependent subdivisions with distinct production processes but with boundaries that are fluid (Glazer 1984). The way each sector goes about reproducing itself involves mutual reliance on the other sectors, perpetuating *their* existences, and in turn—though for the most part unintentionally—that of capitalist society as a whole. At the same time as the sectors are reliant on one another, each sector has interests that are at odds with the others, resulting in conflict. Furthermore, there are tensions within each sector, as firms must compete with other firms for their survival and workers compete with other workers for theirs.

The capitalist firm must compete with other firms, both for the supply of workers and in the market selling commodities. The firm does this by driving down costs and by reinvesting profits to perpetuate its own existence. Firms must hire workers to produce commodities, and firms pay wages to the workers that are equal to the value of the commodity labor-power. Because the value of the commodity labor-power is less than the value of the commodities produced by these workers during the working day, the firm realizes surplus value in the form of profit when the commodities are sold. Contra traditional Marxism (see O'Kane 2018), exploitation described in this way is not "theft" by capitalist firms of surplus value that rightfully belongs to workers. Rather, workers—as they are forced to compete with one another for jobs—are being paid the market price of the commodity labor-power that they are compelled to sell to capitalists (Heinrich 2012). The market price of labor-power is equal to the money price of the commodities used as inputs into the household production function, though this price may be higher or lower depending on the portion of the household's subsistence provided by inputs from the state and the unwaged work of household members. Firms contribute to accumulation by purchasing commodities from other firms as inputs into their production processes. The firm contributes to social reproduction by remitting payments to the state in the form of taxes. The firm also contributes to social reproduction by paying wages and providing other benefits to workers, who use the money from this wage to buy commodities needed for inputs into the household production process to reproduce labor-power.

The state contributes to accumulation by purchasing commodities from firms, which realizes surplus value in the form of profit. The state provides infrastructures that are necessary for both household production and production of commodities by capitalist firms. The state generates laws and their enforcement—such as property rights, contract law, and protections for workers. The state provides welfare goods and services to households that serve as inputs into the household production process, and thus reduces the amount of money wages that firms must pay workers. The welfare state and laws to protect worker safety or to limit the length of the working day can be understood not only as interventions to ensure the continued existence of the capitalist class but also to ensure the continued existence of capitalist society as a whole (Clarke 1988; Heinrich 2012).

The household in capitalism contributes to accumulation and is thus is implicated in social reproduction in four main ways. First, household members who are compelled to sell part of their time for wages contribute to accumulation because their wage is less than the value produced with their labor-power over the course of the working day. Second, the household is the primary site in which the next generation of workers is raised, providing the future source of labor-power. Third, the household purchases commodities as inputs into its household production process, and in doing so surplus value is realized in the form of profit. Fourth, household members may have additional unwaged work shifted onto them by the firms from whom they purchase goods and services without a corresponding decrease in the purchase price of those goods or from the state in the form of volunteer work (Glazer 1984, 1993). The household also contributes to social reproduction by remitting payments to the state in the form of taxes, providing labor to the state in the form of military service and other employment in the state sector, and by reproducing the population.

Redistribution to households within the limits prescribed by the imperatives of accumulation in the form of higher wages or more welfare state goods and services may lead to an increased standard of living for households. However, the interdependencies between the state, capitalist firms, and households—through which the continued existence of one ensures the continued existence of the others, and with this the continued existence of capitalist society—mean that such redistribution is not sufficient to change the underlying production processes that together constitute and reproduce capitalist society (Bonefeld 2008, 70). Moreover, an examination of the specific role of household production and social reproduction in capitalist society suggests that these reforms in some cases may have the unintended consequences of increasing unwaged work and environmental devastation while doing nothing to change the underlying household production process.

Household production and its role in social reproduction

The classical theory of wage determination states that the "natural price of labour is that price which is necessary to enable the labourers, one with another, to subsist and to perpetuate their race" (Ricardo 1951 [1817], 93) or, for Marx, that "the value of labor-power is the value of the means of subsistence necessary for the maintenance of its owner" (Marx 1976 [1867], 274). Ricardo writes that the wage is dependent on but not exactly equal to the money price of the commodities the waged worker and her household need to survive, and Marx argues that, at its minimum level of subsistence, the value of the commodity labor-power is "formed by the value of the commodities which have to be supplied every day to the bearer of labor-power, the man, so that he can renew his life-process" (Marx 1976 [1867], 276). However, in making the simplifying jump from the means of subsistence generically to the value of commodities specifically, both Ricardo and Marx bypass the fact that commodities must be transformed through a household production process in order to be enjoyed by their end users in the household (Reid 1934, 14). The quantity of unwaged work spent in household production is dynamic as both a substitute for and complement to commodities purchased with money from waged labor, and thus also impacts the range of the ultimate and minimum levels of the value of labor-power in terms of commodities.

According to Quick (2018), the wage is not exactly equal to the full amount of labor time necessary for the production and reproduction of labor-power because of the unwaged time that household members spend in household production. State programs such as public education, healthcare, and other welfare state benefits also contribute to the non-equivalence of the worker's wage and the worker's subsistence level (Conference of Socialist Economists 1977, 4). Just as the wage is not static, the quantity of unwaged household labor and the quantity of welfare state benefits involved in the subsistence of households are not static. However, changes in these quantities do not change the underlying household production process or the production processes of capitalist firms, though they may change the standard of living enjoyed by these households within the limits set by the imperative of accumulation. This section of the chapter delves deeper into the process through which households transform resources to produce the intermediate goods that serve as inputs into the production and reproduction of labor-power, and ultimately to the reproduction of capitalist society as a whole.

Households are a single person or multiple people living together in a shared dwelling who share the responsibilities for meeting one another's needs on a day-to-day basis (Netting et al 1984). Household members may or may not be biologically related or related via romantic partnerships, and they may be any gender or no gender at all. Households may contain people across multiple stages of the lifecycle living together, or only one lifecycle stage. Household members may engage in supportive activities within or between households, but they may also have interests that are not aligned or act in ways that are damaging to other household members, for example through conflicts over household resources, domestic violence, or rape. Most households contain at least one member who sells part of her time for wages, but these households may also consist of formerly waged workers or people who would like to work for wages but are unable to find waged employment. Most household members will need to spend at least part of their time engaged in unwaged activities related to household production.

All production involves the transformation of resources into something new that meets the wants or needs of people, and these resources must be combined in some fashion for the transformation of the original inputs to occur. Households in capitalism are constrained by market wages, prices of commodities, the hours in the day, and the goods and services offered by the state. The neoclassical literature on household production is usually presented in terms of partial equilibrium models in which wages and prices are taken as exogenous and state inputs are not included at all. It does not look beyond the single household to system-level processes that determine the levels of prices, wages, or state inputs into household production. Critically adapting Becker (1981) to a Marxist-feminist framework, inputs in this model are both substitutes and complements in the household production process and can be used in varying proportions for the production of household wants and needs. In contrast to Becker, these varying proportions are not determined via a constrained maximization equation on the basis of market and shadow prices. Instead, how household production is carried out—and what goods and services are produced in the household—will depend on know-how, customs, habits, expectations, culture, and the availability of resources. In capitalism, households can be thought of as relying on three main inputs into their household production process: the unwaged efforts of household members, commodities—both goods and services—purchased from the market using money from waged work, and goods and services provided by the state either on a collective or individual basis. As I will show in Chapter 4, households also rely on resources obtained from extended family and friends, nonprofits, theft, and gleaning.

Contrary to theories that see the household as primarily a site of consumption, here households do not consume either commodities or state inputs directly to satisfy their wants and needs. As Reid (1934, 14) points out, "Money income will in itself satisfy few wants; goods in the retail store are not yet available for use." Rather, household members must transform these commodities into the goods and services they enjoy via a household production process. In fact, even the act of gathering commodities that will serve as inputs into household production requires the unwaged time of household members (Weinbaum & Bridges 1976). Goods and services produced in the household for members include comfort, cleanliness, nutrition, safety, health, education, entertainment, and cultural or religious training.[4] Seen this way, the commodities purchased with money from waged work represent derived demand—they are desired not for their own sake, but as inputs into the household production process of the final-use goods and services enjoyed by household members. These final-use goods and services are themselves intermediate goods. According to Quick (2018), the household does not produce just use-values, but rather the intermediate goods and services akin to the intermediate goods produced by a firm that serve as inputs into the final product it sells. One final output of these household production processes is the day-to-day and intergenerational reproduction of workers who are compelled to sell a portion of their time for wages—the commodity labor-power.

The unwaged efforts of household members may include activities such as gathering supplies, transportation, looking after nonworkers, raising children (some of whom may be the next generation of workers), preparing food, transmission of knowledge and skills, cleaning oneself and one's environment, and maintenance or making repairs. But each of these activities involving unwaged work also require additional inputs. Goods and services purchased with wages may include commodities in the form of durable tools and equipment such as automobiles or washing machines, non-durable commodities that are used up in the production process such as yogurt or soap, and the waged time of non-household members who provide services such as a babysitting or curbside trash pickup. Inputs from the state may include infrastructures such as roads or the electrical grid, income insurance, public education, healthcare, and laws and their enforcement.

These inputs are both substitutes and complements in the household production process. They must always be combined but can be relied on in varying proportions as the household manages its resources. Additional unwaged work can be a substitute for commodities purchased with wages in the household production process, or state inputs for market commodities, or state inputs for unwaged work. For example, I can purchase premixed microwave instant oatmeal in a disposable container that requires relatively little unwaged time to gather, cook, clean, and discard. Alternatively, I can purchase for far less money bulk ingredients for traditional oatmeal, which will take more unwaged time to gather, cook, clean, and discard. I can look after an elderly relative with dementia using my own unwaged time, I could pay a waged worker for this service using money earned from waged work, or I could rely on the state to provide eldercare services. In household production, there is frequently more than one way to skin a cat. My informants get things done in everyday life with the resources available to them and subject to the factors—such as limited time, limited money, and cultural considerations—that constrain them in how they go about the household production process but also what end-use goods and services they produce.

Wants, needs, and the "basket of goods"

What goods and services a household produces to meet the needs of its members is dynamic, just as the selection of inputs is dynamic. The components in the "basket of goods" that comprises the subsistence standard of living for a household have changed considerably over time. Wages can be thought of as representing the money price of the commodities a worker uses as an input, along with unwaged work and state-provided inputs, into the production of this basket. The changing components of this basket—and the variations over time and context in methods used by the household to produce the basket—add an additional layer of complexity to a theory of household production. The "basic survival needs" of a household are dependent on customs, habits, expectations, cultural context, infrastructures, and existing or available technologies (Marx 1976 [1867], 275; Stirati 1992).

"Need is a social category" (Adorno 1942, 1). What the household produces and how it goes about that production through routinized activities also depends on what intermediate goods are viewed as culturally necessary and what production processes are viewed as culturally acceptable. While sending newborn babies to wet nurses was widely viewed as the most appropriate way to raise a young child in 18th-century France for all but the most impoverished households, state-funded crèches may be viewed as the best site for childcare in some contexts, while full-time care and extended breastfeeding from stay-at-home mothers practicing attachment parenting may be seen as the best way to raise a child by others (Badinter 1981)—each method requires a different proportion of unwaged labor, inputs purchased with money from waged labor, and state inputs. "Routinized needs and wants" are socially constructed (Shove 2003, 7), are not static, and can be met in a variety of ways. Some of the biggest changes my informants are making in how they get things done in everyday life aren't about swapping out conventional for "green" inputs into the household production process, but rather changing their expectations for what sorts of goods and services are necessary for a good life, and getting by with less.

Technological progress and the expansion of the "basket of goods" are not always good for household members or the environment. New tools and technologies that purport to be unwaged labor-saving devices frequently create new types of unwaged work and new expectations about who should be doing that work, at what site, on what scale, and with what frequency. For example, the introduction of vacuum cleaners changed expectations about floor cleanliness, increased the frequency of floor-cleaning, and shifted that unwaged work onto women—work (rug-beating) that had previously been done infrequently and primarily by men and children (Cowan 1983). "Consumption ratcheting" or the tendency for this household "basket of goods" to grow over time also has particular environmental consequences (cf. Schnaiberg & Gould 1994; Shove & Warde 2002) that should be considered prior to advocating for wage increases and an expansion of household "needs" as the primary short-term goal of class struggle.

Besides, "[i]f production were instantly and without restriction converted into the satisfaction of needs—the satisfaction even, and precisely, of those needs produced by capitalism itself—the needs themselves would therewith be crucially changed" (Adorno 1942, 4). Many of my informants believe that the world they live in is not designed to meet their needs, and indeed frequently feels hostile to their well-being and the well-being of the environment. I will show over the course of this book that these eco-conscious households are rethinking "needs" altogether—from what it means to be comfortable indoors during hot or cold weather, to how many clothes a person should have, to what cleanliness looks or feels like.

A caveat

The reproduction of labor-power has been carried out in a variety of ways during the history of capitalism (Vogel 2013 [1983], 154). The imperative of accumulation means that capital must "tend to socialise (that is turn into a collective activity) the general conditions of capitalist accumulation" (Cockburn 1977, 63). One thing that is not clear is whether the unwaged work that goes into this transformation of commodities into final use-values by the working class and the reproduction of labor-power, when unwaged, more generally represents a subsidy to the capitalist class that allows for the realization of higher profits. Some authors, for example, Lise Vogel (2013 [1983], 162) suggest that there is no subsidy involved, and in fact that *reductions* in domestic labor may *increase* surplus value. Others, such as Dalla Costa and James (1972), suggest that unwaged work does represent a subsidy to the capitalist class. If Lise Vogel's analysis is correct, then from the perspective of the capitalist class, unproductive work involved in reproducing labor-power "is simultaneously indispensable and an obstacle to accumulation" (Vogel 2013 [1983], 163).

Furthermore, labor-power can be replenished via other means—such as proletarianization—and in other sites, such as schools, "labour-camps, barracks, orphanages, hospitals, prisons, and other such institutions" (Vogel 2013 [1983], 159). Couldn't housing workers in barracks and raising children in giant company-run nurseries be more cost-effective for capitalist firms thanks to economies of scale? Indeed, both Michèle Barrett (1980) and Michael Heinrich (2011 [1999]) point out that it is not obvious why the configuration of people and production into nuclear family households would be one favored by capitalists. As Cynthia Cockburn (1977, 102) puts it, "when we identify the advantages to the state and capitalism in a certain course of action, when we look for possible motives, it seems to imply that some mastermind is at work—foreseeing, planning, and pre-empting. The truth is not like this, as daily practice makes more than clear."

It may be tempting to see all the everyday practices of household members in capitalism as contributing to accumulation either directly or indirectly, designed to maximize surplus value as if there is some mastermind at work. Once we start picking apart our supposedly pro-environmental activities, such as recycling sorting (Munro 2022), or buying fair-trade coffee (Doane 2010), or selecting "green energy" suppliers (Dunlap 2019; Mulvaney 2019), we can begin to trace the links between our mundane practices and the imperative of accumulation in everything we do. And it is true that many of the easily overlooked activities that constitute our everyday lives in capitalism contribute to the continued existence of capitalism—buying food to eat, going to school, going to work, and raising children to be "good citizens." In capitalism, labor-power is reproduced capitalistically, and my theoretical model indicates that household production in capitalism is inextricably linked to capitalist production.

However, I believe it is reductive to portray everything about the way we get things done in everyday life as if it were maximally beneficial to the capitalist class, our preferences entirely the result of deceptive advertising and trickery.[5] The capitalist class does not care if you sweep your floors once a day or once a month or never. Every single activity that people do with their children isn't deliberately selected to maximize future exploitability. If waged workers can "strike on the job" (Hill 2015 [1914], 32) and intentionally waste time and resources, then certainly unwaged workers engaged in household production can participate in activities that do not directly benefit the capitalist class or contribute to the continued existence of capitalism. Many of our mundane practices can be thought of as rituals, habits, and customs—"preferences" and ways of getting things done that are determined culturally and socially—which, from the perspective of accumulation, are pointless.

Conclusion

Describing mundane practices in eco-conscious households in Portland, Oregon, and their meanings for practitioners—my informants—makes up the bulk of this book. This chapter has been a theoretical detour into the Marxist-feminist model of household production that I developed to better understand why so many of my informants tell me they feel frustrated, exhausted, and like their hands are tied when it comes to promoting the well-being of their household members and the environment. The three-sector model I presented here differs from progressive/liberal feminist economics and the new Marxist-feminist offshoot Social Reproduction Theory for two key reasons. First, this model does not emphasize the gendered distribution of waged and unwaged work or the assignment of money, credit, or recognition for that work. Second, this model emphasizes the links between household production and the reproduction of capitalist society, demonstrating that the household is complicit in the reproduction of capitalist society.

Household production plays a necessary role in the reproduction of capitalist society, and the interdependencies between the production that takes place in households, firms, and the state in capitalism mean that these sectors are inextricably linked to one another via their inputs and outputs—the household is not a sanctuary outside capitalism. I have argued that household production can take place using varying proportions of inputs, but that changing the proportions of these inputs does not change the underlying production process let alone the organization of capitalist society. This model leads me to conclude that the reproduction of labor-power that takes place in households and elsewhere cannot be divorced from the reproduction of capitalist society, nor from the human and environmental disasters inherent to it. These conclusions help me understand why so many of my ecologically conscious informants feel exhausted, frustrated, guilty, and as if none of their pro-environmental interventions are actually making a difference.

My critique of production—including household production—in capitalism suggests a different set of questions that motivate this research than those that might be advanced by feminist economics or Social Reproduction Theory. What are "needs," how are needs determined, and what determines the components of the "basket of goods" that meets these needs? What other methods, sites, and scales could be employed to meet the needs of people? Is, as Nancy Folbre asserts, "love" what is missing from previous models of household production (Folbre 1994, 15)? Are, as Tithi Bhattacharya contends, waged and unwaged labor the sources of all wealth (Bhattacharya 2017, 1)? Or, is this love and labor—and the capitalist production and reproduction processes that employ them—simply means of reproducing the social reality outlined in this chapter, which inhibits the further development of all of those people alive today and that threatens the very existence of the planet and future generations?

References

Adorno, Theodor (1942) "Theses on Need," translated by Keston Sutherland, Available: http://freudians.org/wp-content/uploads/2015/08/theodor-w-adorno-theses-on-need-1.pdf [Accessed April 11, 2021].

Arruzza, Cinzia (2016) "Functionalist, determinist, reductionist: Social reproduction feminism and its critics," *Science & Society*, 80(1): 9–30.

Badinter, Elisabeth (1981) *Mother Love. Myth and Reality: Motherhood in Modern History*, New York: Macmillan.

Barrett, Michèle (1980) *Women's Oppression Today: Problems in Marxist Feminist Analysis*, London: Verso.

Becker, Gary S. (1981) *A Treatise on the Family*, Cambridge, MA: Harvard University Press.

Bhattacharya, Tithi (2017) "Introduction," in Tithi Bhattacharya (ed) *Social Reproduction Theory: Remapping Class, Recentering Oppression*, London: Pluto Press, pp 1–20.

Bonefeld, Werner (2008) "Global capital, national state, and the international," *Critique*, 36(1): 63–72.

Chiswick, Carmel U. (1999) "The economics of Jewish continuity," *Contemporary Jewry*, 20(1): 30–56.

Chiswick, Carmel U. and Barry R. Chiswick (2000) "The cost of living Jewishly and Jewish continuity," *Contemporary Jewry*, 21(1): 78–90.

Clarke, Simon (1988) *Keynesianism, Monetarism, and the Crisis of the State*, Aldershot: Edward Elgar.

Clarke, Simon (1994) *Marx's Theory of Crisis*, Houndmills: Macmillan.

Cockburn, Cynthia (1977) *The Local State: Management of Cities and People*, London: Pluto Press.

Collins, Jane L. (1990) "Unwaged labor in comparative perspective: Recent theories and unanswered questions," in Jane L. Collins and Martha Giménez (eds) *Work without Wages: Comparative Studies of Domestic Labor and Self-Employment*, Albany: State University of New York Press, pp 3–24.

Conference of Socialist Economists (1977) *On the Political Economy of Women*, CSE Pamphlet No. 2, London: Stage 1.

Cowan, Ruth Schwarz (1983) *More Work for Mother: The Ironies of Household Technologies from the Open Hearth to the Microwave*, New York: Basic Books.

Dalla Costa, Mariarosa and Selma James (1972) *The Power of Women and the Subversion of the Community*, Bristol: Falling Wall Press.

Doane, Molly (2010) "Relationship coffees: Structure and agency in the fair trade system," in Sarah Lyon (ed) *Fair Trade and Social Justice: Global Ethnographies*, New York: New York University Press, pp 229–257.

Dunlap, Alexander (2019) *Renewing Destruction: Wind Energy Development, Conflict and Resistance in a Latin American Context*, London: Rowman & Littlefield.

Ferber, Marianne A. and Julie A. Nelson (eds) (2009) *Beyond Economic Man: Feminist Theory and Economics*, Chicago: University of Chicago Press.

Ferguson, Susan (2019) *Women and Work: Feminism, Labour, and Social Reproduction*, London: Pluto Press.

Folbre, Nancy (1994) *Who Pays for the Kids? Gender and the Structures of Constraint*, London: Routledge.

Giménez, Martha (1990) "Waged work, domestic labor and household survival in the United States," in Jane L. Collins and Martha Giménez (eds) *Work without Wages: Comparative Studies of Domestic Labor and Self-Employment within Capitalism*, Albany: State University of New York Press, pp 25–46.

Giménez, Martha (2018) *Marx, Women, and Capitalist Social Reproduction: Marxist-Feminist Essays*, Boston, MA: Brill.

Glazer, Nona Y. (1984) "Servants to capital: Unpaid domestic labor and paid work," *Review of Radical Political Economics*, 16(1): 61–87.

Glazer, Nona Y. (1993) *Women's Paid and Unpaid Labor: The Work Transfer in Health Care and Retailing*, Philadelphia, PA: Temple University Press.

Heinrich, Michael (2011 [1999]) *Die Wissenschaft vom Wert*, Münster: Westfälisches Dampfboot.

Heinrich, Michael (2012) *An Introduction to the Three Volumes of Karl Marx's Capital*, New York: Monthly Review Press.

Hicks, John R. and R. G. D. Allen (1934) "A reconsideration of the theory of value: Part I," *Economica*, 1(1): 52–76.

Hill, Joe (2015 [1914]) "How to make work for the unemployed," in Philip S. Foner (ed) *The Letters of Joe Hill*, Chicago: Haymarket Books, pp 28–33.

Marx, Karl (1976 [1867]) *Capital: Volume I*, translated by Ben Fowkes, London: Penguin Books.

Mosak, Jacob L. (1938) "Interrelations of production, price, and derived demand," *Journal of Political Economy*, 46(6): 761–787.

Mulvaney, Dustin (2019) *Solar Power: Innovation, Sustainability, and Environmental Justice*, Oakland: University of California Press.

Munro, Kirstin (2019) "'Social Reproduction Theory', social reproduction, and household production," *Science & Society*, 83(4): 451–468.

Munro, Kirstin (2022) "Overaccumulation, crisis, and the contradictions of household waste sorting," *Capital & Class* 46(1): 115–131.

Netting, Robert, Richard R. Wilk, and Eric J. Arnould (1984) "Introduction," in Robert Netting, Richard R. Wilk, and Eric J. Arnould (eds) *Households: Comparative and Historical Studies of the Domestic Group*, Berkeley: University of California Press.

O'Kane, Chris (2018) "Moishe Postone's new reading of Marx: The critique of political economy as a critical theory of the historically specific social form of labor," *Consecutio Rerum*, 5.

O'Kane, Chris and Kirstin Munro (2022). "Marxian economics and the Critique of Political Economy," in Werner Bonefeld and Chris O'Kane (eds) *Adorno and Marx: Negative Dialectics and the Critique of Political Economy*, London: Bloomsbury, pp 77–95.

Quick, Paddy (2018) "Labor power: A 'peculiar' commodity," *Science & Society*, 82(3): 386–412.

Reid, Margaret (1934) *The Economics of Household Production*, New York: John Wiley & Sons, Inc.

Ricardo, David (1951 [1817]) *On the Principles of Political Economy and Taxation*, Indianapolis: Liberty Fund.

Schnaiberg, Allan and Kenneth Alan Gould (1994) *Environment and Society: The Enduring Conflict*, Caldwell, NJ: Blackburn Press.

Shove, Elizabeth (2003) *Comfort, Cleanliness, and Convenience: The Social Organization of Normality*, Oxford: Berg.

Shove, Elizabeth and Alan Warde (2002) "Inconspicuous consumption: The sociology of consumption, lifestyles, and the environment," in Riley E. Dunlap, Frederick H. Buttel, Peter Dickens, and August Gijswijt (eds) *Sociological Theory and the Environment: Classical Foundations, Contemporary Insights*, Oxford: Rowman & Littlefield, pp 230–251.

Stirati, Antonella (1992) "Institutions, unemployment and the living standard in the classical theory of wages," *Contributions to Political Economy*, 11: 41–66.

Trotsky, Leon (2002 [1938]) *The Death Agony of Capitalism and the Tasks of the Fourth International. The Mobilization of the Masses around Transitional Demands to Prepare for the Conquest of Power: The Transitional Program*, Available from: https://www.marxists.org/archive/trotsky/1938/tp/trans program.pdf [Accessed September 21, 2022].

Vogel, Lise (2013 [1983]) *Marxism and the Oppression of Women: Toward a Unitary Theory*, Leiden: Koninklijke Brill.

Weeks, Kathi (2011) *The Problem with Work: Feminism, Marxism, Antiwork Politics, and Postwork Imaginaries*, Durham, NC: Duke University Press.

Weinbaum, Batya and Amy Bridges (1976) "The other side of the paycheck: Monopoly capital and the structure of consumption," *Monthly Review*, 28(3): 88–101.

3

Priorities in
Eco-Conscious Households

The 23 households I met with over the course of the spring in 2017 were more different from each other than I initially expected. I had assumed that sustainability in Portland, Oregon, would be a largely liberal White upper-middle-class phenomenon, and that the practices would primarily serve as conspicuous forms of class distinction and display. However, the informants and households I spoke with represented more diversity than I anticipated—in personal backgrounds, household configurations, socioeconomic status, political leanings, education, race and ethnicity, and the gender of the householders.

Despite these differences, the adults in these households share a common, sincerely held desire to do the right thing for their children, households, communities, and planet. My informants try to make decisions for their households and balance their sustainability priorities with constrained resources, which often involves fairly major interventions into conventional ways of getting things done in order to bring their everyday practices into alignment with their values. I learned that there is not a single "sustainability," with households engaging in sustainability practices to varying degrees of intensity along a green spectrum. Rather, sustainability represents a broad set of values and beliefs for these Portland households, with sustainability practices influenced by the unique combinations of priorities, resources, and constraints in each household.

Mike and Mina have two large cars that they use for long daily drives from their suburban home to their various obligations. For Mina, whose Middle Eastern extended family lives nearby, the primary focus in the sustainability realm is the health of herself and her family members. For this reason, she makes her own natural deodorant, gives her children alternative remedies like elderberry syrup, and prepares elaborate home-cooked vegetarian meals with organic ingredients she buys during her frequent trips to far-flung grocery stores. As a stay-at-home mother, she sees her unpaid time as her major contribution to the household. David and Dayna, on the other hand, are both White professionals who work in downtown Portland. They own only one car and commute to their daily obligations almost exclusively by bicycle, including dropping their infant child off at daycare. They have government-subsidized solar panels and energy-efficiency devices in their home, but they eat a lot of frozen convenience foods and takeout meals since becoming parents. They pride themselves on their self-sufficiency. Technology and electronic gadgets are the primary focus of their sustainability practices; they see these as solutions to environmental problems. Leonda, a Black, gender nonbinary person who uses she/her and they/them pronouns, bikes to their position as an AmeriCorps volunteer, practices selective flushing, and was so committed to cloth diapering that they handwashed diapers in the bathtub when they were living in an apartment without access to laundry facilities. However, they find it difficult to learn how to make healthy meals for their family since they grew up eating mostly fast food, a habit they are trying to break, and their Supplemental Nutrition Program for Women, Infants, and Children (WIC) food benefits have restrictions that prevent them from using the funds to buy natural food items. Growing up in a heavily contaminated region of Appalachia, Leonda's primary sustainability concerns are environmental justice and the community impacts of corporate pollution.

In each of these cases, my informants balance their resources and constraints to produce sustainability practices in their households that prioritize the things they care about the most. This chapter will introduce you to my informants: their families of origin, what they see as the source of their current sustainability values and practices, their current living arrangements and household structures, and their priorities and motivations for their sustainability practices. The overlapping sustainability priorities of the households in this study include community well-being, the health of individual family members, nature, technology, and waste avoidance. Chapter 4 will describe household resources and constraints in more detail.

Introducing my informants

Families of origin

How my informants grew up often had a significant influence on their current priorities and practices. For some informants, particularly ones who were raised by countercultural or highly thrift-oriented parents, this is because the habits and values of their families of origin were carried forward into their current lives. For others, their practices and values as adults were formed in contraposition to those of their families of origin, a theme that was prevalent for informants who described their childhoods as typically suburban and their parents as excessively invested in consumer culture. Informants who retained resource-conserving practices they had learned from their parents often attributed those habits to their upbringing. For example, Chris likes to wash out and reuse plastic bags, something his countercultural parents did faithfully. However, more conventional ways of getting things done, such as owning two cars or eating microwaved food, were rarely explained by my informants as habits and values learned from their own parents. Tara, a particularly self-aware and reflective informant, was an exception, as she attributes her positive associations with and desire for consumer goods to her conventional upbringing and the materialistic values of her parents.

Chris, Carrie, Fiona, Jim, and Scott were raised by parents with strong links to the 1960 and 1970s hippy counterculture and environmental activism. Chris recalls hang-drying clothes and occasionally bringing them inside frozen during the winter, and his wife Carrie was raised in a spiritual intentional community that impressed upon her a belief in the importance of bearing in mind her impact on other people. Fiona and Jim were raised by parents influenced by Back-to-the-Land ideals, though they both remarked on the shifting emphasis as their parents aged, with an increased value placed on comfort and convenience. Scott's parents were involved in early pro-environmental litigation and activism, though he commented on an incongruity between the environmental values of his parents and many of their personal habits and choices.

Other informants were raised by more conventional parents. Gloria, Jess, Owen, Penny, and Tara see themselves as rebelling against the excessive consumerism and emphasis on material goods from their suburban moderate-income families of origin. Owen describes his childhood as "Midwestern Leave it to Beaver," and talks about air conditioning as something households in his community growing up would install to show their neighbors that they'd "made it." Gloria says that her mother's materialistic values were based in shame and a need to prove her worth as a single parent through buying things. Tara still struggles occasionally with the linkage, instilled by her family of origin, between love and consumer goods. Penny recalls a Midwestern suburban home so large that her family members had to yell across the house to communicate with each other. As an adult, she finds it odd that her parents' home was climate controlled to the same temperature year-round.

Leonda and Heather were both raised by low-income single mothers and left their family homes prior to graduating high school. Heather sees herself as a strong and independent person because she had to be so responsible for herself and her siblings growing up. She contrasts herself as a parent with her mother by saying they have different priorities for how they spend their time. Leonda recalls their grandmother, who partially raised them, teaching them how to apply for food stamps and other government benefits as a teenager in Appalachia. Ivy was raised in a low-income and highly religious family in a manufactured home in Central Oregon. While her husband complimented Ivy's mother for her resourcefulness and thrift, the parallels between her mother's life skills and her own were less obvious to Ivy, who sees her adult lifestyle as a rebellion against her mother's consumerism and desire for comfort.

While Kyle, Nathan, Orla, Tim, and Yvonne also grew up in low-income households, they described thrift as a guiding principle for their parents that was independent of their financial status. Kyle's father died when he was young, leaving his mother to raise him and his siblings alone. He expressed gratitude for his mother's resourcefulness, and he appreciated her decision to live without a car in a medium-sized Midwestern city. Yvonne also told me that she appreciates the skills and resilience she and her husband learned growing up in low-income families as well as the food storage equipment they receive as gifts from her husband's Church of Jesus Christ of Latter Day Saints (Mormon) parents. Tim's parents are members of a strict religious sect who believe in an impending Biblical End Times. According to their faith, Tim's family were among the meek who would inherit the earth, so they were extremely thrifty and mindful of the natural environment—they did not want to spend the rest of eternity cleaning up after people who were not saved. Nathan's father was a minister and his parents were Christian progressives who were involved in Vietnam War protests and the early environmental movement. Nathan was taught by his father to fix everything and waste nothing, and these values have been carried forward to his present lifestyle and habits. Jim wonders in hindsight if his father's thrift and pro-environmental behaviors were purely based on ethical choices, or were also motivated by raising two children on his own with few financial resources. Orla's father continues to live an extremely thrifty lifestyle, recently spending some years collecting old pallets off the side of the road until he had collected enough wood to build himself a new work shed.

Origins of sustainability values and practices

While the households in this book come from diverse cultural and socioeconomic backgrounds, the importance of personal contacts in influencing my informants' current values and practices in the sustainability realm was almost universal. Fiona credits her siblings with many of her sustainability practices—she became a vegetarian when her brother showed her that eating meat wasn't necessary, and she started flushing the toilet selectively after living with her sister and realizing she didn't have to flush the toilet after urinating. Leonda did not have any sustainability-oriented contacts until they were in their teens, but began turning off lights in unoccupied rooms after seeing an energy conservation public service announcement on television and started flushing selectively after watching the 2004 movie *Meet the Fockers*, which has a scene about "letting it mellow." Many of Leonda's other practices and values were picked up from environmental activists in their community who were a few years older than they were, whom they met through their Unitarian Universalist faith community. Similarly, Tara was influenced by older people in her profession who she met after moving away from home—people who made deliberate ethical consumption choices and ate more nutritious foods than she had been exposed to growing up in a Mexican–American household in Southern California. Dayna says a close friend with similar values convinced her that she could use cloth diapers, and reduced the burden of research by teaching her and giving her information about why and how to use the diapers. Mina was a fairly conventional suburban Southern California parent prior to moving to Portland and sending her children to a cooperative preschool. Now that she has adopted some of the sustainability practices of the other parents from her preschool, her old friends jokingly tell her that she's become a hippy.

Education, particularly postsecondary education, also played an important role in influencing the environmental and social values of several informants. Chris, Emily, Fiona, Heather, Owen, and Penny all had meaningful experiences with university coursework that influenced their current worldviews. Emily believes that her environmental science education is a privilege that enables her to be aware of sustainability issues and the possible health impacts on her family members, and she recognizes that not all families have the same ability to access and process health information. Fiona and Penny share a conviction that their interdisciplinary environmental science educations helped them understand how their actions impact ecosystems and people living in less developed countries. Owen had a conventional White Midwestern upbringing, and a nature photography class that brought him to Oregon introduced him to environmental issues and the importance and beauty of the natural environment. Chris took a class about environmental crises when he was 19 that he called "a body-blow of a class where I was so depressed afterwards." Even though he was raised by unconventional environmentalist parents, he credits this class with shaping his worldview and the way he lives his life today.

The sustainability-oriented households in my sample had considerable variation in terms of the political affiliations and beliefs motivating their sustainability values and practices, with beliefs that sometimes even diverged within individual couples. Some amount of homogeneity in the political beliefs and sustainability motivations is to be expected in a sample deliberately drawn from a single, highly liberal, racially homogenous metro area. Informants volunteered to participate in my study based on their self-identification as members of an eco-conscious or sustainable household, but belief in climate change and environmental concern are increasingly a matter of social group knowledge, with wide divergence in the opinions of Democrats and Republicans (Dunlap & McCright 2008). However, my informants included anticapitalist socialists, democratic socialists, moderate Republicans confused by the recent election of Donald Trump, vaguely libertarian moderates, moderate Democrats, left-of-center progressive Democrats, Green Party voters, and even one informant who described his overall value system using concepts such as "White replacement" that are linked to White supremacy, eco-fascism, and the so-called alt-right.

From the far right or far left or somewhere in between, the sustainability-oriented households I spoke with described their lifestyles as deliberately constructed in opposition to particular elements of mainstream U.S. culture that they oppose: individualism, consumerism, wastefulness and a lack of gratitude, technology and social media, instant gratification, selfishness, and the loss of traditional values. A national sample of households engaging in these practices might include even greater variation in motivations and political beliefs driving sustainability practices. While there is no ethnographic social practices research on U.S. households that I could use for a comparison "control group" to my households, their perspective was clear—they view their sustainability practices as an alternative to what they see as conventional American ways of getting things done.

Current living arrangements and family structures

Of the 23 households in the sample, 13 comprised people living in a nuclear family with two parents in a heterosexual relationship, their related children, and no other people. However, the remaining ten households represented other configurations of people living together, including a lesbian couple, a couple in which one of the members is gender nonbinary, intentional communal living arrangements with nonrelated people, single parents, blended families, roommates, and extended families. The full list of household configurations is available in Table 3.1.

Many foundational theories discussing work and households in the context of an advanced industrialized society presuppose a particular household arrangement—two parents, a man who engages in paid work outside the home and a woman who does not, living in the same space as their biological children. This type of living arrangement, the joining of kinship and heterosexual cohabitation, may be promoted by the state and other institutions as the ideal, but it is a modern one that was at no time universal in industrialized countries (Barrett 1980, 200–204; Netting et al 1984; Collins 2000 [1990], 45–68; Munro 2021). My sample, like the real world, includes a diverse array of household configurations.

Household sustainability priorities

The households in this study were self-selected on the basis of their own perception that their values and practices have a sustainability or pro-environmental orientation. However, the sustainability priorities and practices in

Table 3.1: Sample household configurations

Description	Number
Nuclear family with two parents in a heterosexual relationship	13
Nuclear family with two parents in a lesbian relationship	1
Single parent, children present part-time	2
Single parent, children present full-time	1
Blended family, children present full-time	1
Blended family, children present part-time	1
Nuclear family with two parents, one male and one gender nonbinary, and one adult roommate	1
Nuclear family with two parents in a heterosexual relationship and one grandparent	1
Nuclear family with two parents in a heterosexual relationship, one grandparent, and additional nonrelated family in intentional community	1
Nuclear family with two parents in a heterosexual relationship in cohousing community	1

these households were not variations along a single "green" spectrum. Rather, households had sustainability priorities related to personal health, nature, waste, technology, and community. Households' priorities generally consisted of two or three of these sustainability realms, with one facet of sustainability generally standing out as the primary concern. Another difference between households was whether the motivation for an informant's sustainability interests was primarily oriented toward household members or people, animals, and ecosystems external to the household. Households with priorities related to personal health, waste, and technology tended to have a more internal orientation in their motivations, while households who were most concerned with nature and community tended to have a more external motivation. This section discusses these household sustainability priorities in more detail.

Personal health

Households whose sustainability priority is *personal health* are worried about contamination, specifically with chemicals, and the impacts of chemicals on the health of their children and themselves.

Emily: I don't want my kids to be exposed to chemicals. I certainly value the environment second to my family of all my priorities in life, but the health of the kids is the primary driver of these decisions for me.

"Chemicals" is a very vague term that my informants use to talk about properties of foods, additives, and medicines that are not "natural." Informants whose sustainability priority is personal health distrust large corporations, conventional medicine and the medical field, and the government and associated regulatory bodies.

Yvonne: I don't want to sound like a conspiracy theorist, but I don't really trust the government. It's been proven time and time again that money prevails. It is constantly being shown that we are the last ones to know about things being done that are adverse for our health. To get anywhere in politics, politicians have to put companies before people because that's where their money is coming from.

The focus of personal health-related sustainability practices is avoiding potential negative health impacts on people inside the household related to particular purchases, like food items, medications, personal care products, and cleaning products. These informants spend time researching alternative ways of getting things done to avoid chemicals, such as making their own laundry detergent and alternative medical treatments. These interests are not necessarily linked to the environment, but the informants consider them to be part of their sustainability values. Informants with personal health as a priority might not consider the environment in their everyday choices:

Heather: We don't think about saving energy much at all!

Heather has made major interventions into her everyday practices—extended breastfeeding until age four, buying all-organic food, homeschooling her three children, keeping a large food garden and chickens, and making her own cleaning products out of natural ingredients and essential oils. However, larger environmental considerations are off her radar.

While Heather and Amy have medical training and work in the medical field, other health-oriented informants see themselves as amateur researchers and doctors.

Heather: I'm a nurse, so I live in medicine. That's what I do for my profession, but I probably buck against the system as much as I can, against Western medicine. In the sense that when we seek out more natural alternatives that are treating the source of the problem. Not masking [the problem], and not using pharmaceuticals. So, we are not like families who trust that system.

Yvonne calls herself an "amateur herbalist." She uses books to research herbalism, and forages for treatments for her son's severe asthma and her own chronic health condition because she is "not comfortable" with the idea of treating these ailments with corticosteroids. Earlier in his life, Victor had wanted to be a doctor. While he ultimately decided on a different career, he retained this interest in medicine and enjoys reading about health and doing nutrition and natural health experiments on his family members.

Given the controversial nature of the subject, none of my informants admitted to having unvaccinated children, nor did I ask about vaccinations. Vanessa mentioned that she thinks children *probably* have all of their vaccinations now, but she used an alternative vaccination schedule. Discussions with Mina and Rebecca, two parents who did fully vaccinate their children, gave the impression that antivaccine sentiment was prevalent among sustainability-oriented households in Portland. Oregon has the highest nonmedical vaccination exception rate in the country, and the Portland Village School, a sustainability-focused Waldorf-inspired public charter school, had a nonmedical vaccination opt-out rate of 53 percent around the time these interviews took place, the highest for a public school in the state (Foden-Vencil 2015). While I conducted these interviews prior to the COVID-19 pandemic and related vaccination politicization and controversies, childhood vaccinations were already contentious for the households I interviewed in 2017.

Mina spoke to me in a whisper when she told me that she knows a quarter of the children in her preschool are unvaccinated. She thinks the other parents would have a negative opinion of her if they knew her children received all their vaccinations on the conventional schedule. Rebecca was less apologetic and was unconcerned with how parents of unvaccinated children perceive her.

Rebecca: My kids are 100 percent vaccinated. I feel that it is a disservice ... no, that's not strong enough of a word. I feel that if you do not vaccinate your child, you should not be allowed to attend public school or take them into public where there are children who are too young or people who are medically fragile and can't get those vaccines. I think people who are not vaccinating their children believe in pseudoscience and believe in personal choice over the public good. And those things seem directly in conflict with being environmentally conscious. Being environmentally conscious is about the public good and creating an environment that is healthy for ALL OF US, as well as believing in the science that tells us that there is a demonstrable shift in our environment based on our human habits. One is pretty anti-science and one is pro-science.

While Rebecca frames this issue as pro-science and anti-science, the health-oriented families I spoke with do not see their views and practices as "anti-science." They devote a considerable amount of effort to researching their choices, and they have concluded that mainstream science and medicine are wrong about certain topics. However, Rebecca does point out an important distinction between her sustainability priorities and the priorities of some personal health-oriented informants: Rebecca's primary concern and motivation for her sustainability practices is public welfare, while personal health-oriented families are most concerned with the well-being of the members of their immediate household.

Nature

Households whose sustainability focus is *nature* express a concern for the environment and ecosystems for their own sake. This concern for the environment is not oriented toward household members and often not toward human beings at all.

Andrew: What we're doing in our house isn't just good for us, it's because we care about the environment in general.

Fiona: I value the planet as a living organism. Even if humans weren't a part of that, I would still want to care for all of the other creatures and ecosystems at large.

Informants for whom nature is a high sustainability priority are concerned with the carbon impacts of their purchases and activities, the impacts of air pollution and effluent, and the welfare of plants and animals.

Jim: For me the preeminent environmental motivator is the carbon impact, and then secondary to that would be the public health impacts.

Some of these households also tied their interest in sustainability to experiences enjoying nature recreationally, and childhood experiences in nature were cited as inspiring their current sustainability interests.

Quinn: Nature was important to my parents, and taking us outside.

Andrew: I became interested in sustainability growing up, I was just exposed to the mountains and to things outside of the city. There's green in the city, too, but I got out into nature just growing up, so I got an appreciation for nature and preserving it.

Eric: My stepdad took me camping a lot, we spent a lot of time in the Sierras [mountain range in California and Nevada], and canoeing around. And that imparted an appreciation for nature that is the underpinning of [my sustainability practices] now.

These experiences in childhood inspired my informants to make efforts to take their children into what they call "nature."

Emily: An appreciation for nature is a big thing for me. We try to get them out into the woods, we take them hiking a lot. Getting them out of the city and trying to instill an appreciation for the natural environment. That's a big priority for us.

Quinn: I think it's important for my kid to get out in nature and appreciate nature, because I hope that when he's older that will mean he will want to do things to help the environment.

They believe that if their children learn to enjoy nature for its recreational value, they will be motivated to have pro-environmental views and practices as adults.

Waste

Households whose sustainability focus is *waste* are concerned about wasting resources because thrift and avoiding wasting resources is an important value in and of itself. This sustainability priority reflects the religious and cultural impulse toward asceticism noted by Weber (2002 [1905], 115) and Bourdieu (1984, 286). Kyrk (1923, 74) describes these impulses in the U.S. context: "Self-sacrifice and deprivation are goods in themselves"—thrift and deprivation are social goods that serve as a display of one's values and good moral character.

Nathan: It's all part of the same philosophy—don't waste shit. Wasting money, wasting anything else. Don't waste a minute, don't waste a dollar, don't waste a thing.

This avoidance of waste particularly applies to energy and the packaging of consumer goods.

Dayna: And that concern about waste, packaging, David has always been more focused on that and that's been more of a mission for him and I've been chastised by him for not doing stuff because I'm just like "Uuuuggh."

Eric: But I hate how everything goes into a container and that's the default in our culture and our stores. Container within container within container. It's so unnecessary.

Quinn: We teach our son about recycling, and to turn off the lights if you're not in the room. We don't have many conversations, but we more teach by example.

The priority of waste avoidance also applies to households who have an interest in "voluntary simplicity," try to buy as little as possible, or avoid buying new consumer goods, reflecting a current trend in U.S. culture of possessing a carefully curated set of only a few just-right items (Bernstein 2016; Chayka 2016; Logan 2017).

Gloria: We have what we need and we need what we have. We try really hard not to frivolously acquire. We try to bring things into the house that have several purposes that are very useful. And I mean that in terms of food, clothing, anything from food to an appliance.

Fiona: We really avoid getting a lot of *things* and just see what we can do with what we have. And that's my approach to everything: how can I use what I already have.

Heather: Less is more. Minimalism in a sense. Though I sometimes feel that it's not possible. We don't really splurge on a whole lot. Whether it means that we're going to the library for our books. "Less is more" also applies to medicine, and we always research what we're doing to make sure it is healthy. And we are working on being more sustainable as far as doing things here, the gardening and the chickens.

Like Heather, Brian admits that voluntary simplicity is often more of a goal than an accurate description of the way he actually lives.

Brian: The one other thing that is more of an aspiration is "simple," just "simple lifestyle."

Some households refer to this value as "thrift" and discuss previous generations' experience during times of poverty, particularly the Great Depression.

Nathan: My parents were Depression kids, so this ethic of "if it doesn't work, fix it" comes from them.

Orla: My dad is what a lot of people would consider cheap. He does not like to waste anything. He has a thirty-year-old fridge, but he doesn't want to get a new one because that would be wasteful. He grew up with parents who were a little bit older, definitely influenced by the Great Depression era.

Kyle: The driver for my mother was being a child of survivors of the Great Depression, and depression-era economics, which she carried on. She had those skills from her childhood which she brought into our household. These are values from close to 100 years ago being moved forward. They were transmitted to my mother and then to me. Economizing, and not taking more than you need, and figuring out how to reuse things. There is a real continuity there that the environmental movement relies on.

These informants see their own values and practices as their inheritance from past experiences of economic crisis in their families of origin.

Technology

Households whose sustainability focus is technology often value technology for its own sake. When asked about the motivations for his interest in sustainability, David answered that enjoying "gadgets" is a major impetus for their pro-environmental practices.

David: For me it's also just gadgets and geeky energy stuff. Like geeky energy stuff, I just enjoy. I'm always looking around like, "What could I do next?"

Some of these informants see their technology purchases as direct expressions of their sustainability values, while others see their interest in technology as conflicting with their sustainability values.

Brian: And I think as much as my ideal self would be living very simply, I do have a bit of a technology … Not quite a fetish, but definitely a predilection … It's something that I can kind of justify by saying it is part of my world, it is part of my job. But the reality is that it's just one of my interests, and it's one of the areas where I kind of think that that kind of simplicity, that buying fewer things, kind of breaks down in my life.

David and Dayna pride themselves on thrift in many areas of their lives, except when it comes to technology.

Dayna:	We are not the kind of people who will do the better option at any price.
David:	Except for some things.
Kirstin:	What's an example of that?
David:	Pretty much any energy-efficiency gadget.

For Brian, David, Dayna, Nathan, and Nicole, technology and energy-efficiency improvements are solutions to environmental problems. Brian has one of the warmer winter temperature settings of my informants, and recently installed a smart thermostat he can control from his computer or phone. This device allows him to prevent the heat turning on automatically when he decides last minute to spend the evening at his new girlfriend's house. David and Dayna see technology—a dual-flush toilet they recently purchased—as a solution that allows them to save water without practicing selective flushing, and they recently changed all of the light switches in their home to motion-sensor switches, because they believed carrying an infant was preventing them from always switching off lights.

| David: | I probably do have a higher tolerance [for selective flushing]. I would go a few more flushes probably, but I think the dual flush toilet solved that problem. |

They also admit that they just find the technology fun and interesting. David and Dayna are evangelical about their robot vacuum cleaner and solar panels. While Nathan calculated the return on investment of his costly geothermal system and decided that it was the most cost-effective way to heat and cool his home, he also refers to the system as a "toy."

Kirstin:	And what was the main motivation behind installing the solar panels?
Dayna:	Because solar is fantastic!
Nathan:	We have geothermal heating and cooling. It is a really high-efficiency rating system. Both radiant floor and forced air. It is totally cool. You've got to see this thing. We are geeks at heart, so the technology is just really exciting. It's a cool toy.
Nicole:	I am more willing to spend money on cool stuff just because it is cool or helpful.

Some of the households I spoke with see technology as a social and environmental problem, something that contributes to wasted resources, escalating consumption, and prevents human intimacy in communities. Despite an awareness of these criticisms, informants with a technology focus believe that technology has a positive role to play in their lives and the world.

Community

Households whose sustainability focus is *community* are concerned with the well-being of people outside their own families—either on a local or global scale—and see their community-oriented lifestyle as an expression of their sustainability values. Sometimes this interest in community is expressed as contrasting with others who are more oriented toward their nuclear families, while for other informants this value of community is a social justice focus. Gloria summarizes her community-oriented sustainability focus by emphasizing that her children are not her sole motivation for environmental choices.

Gloria: Community is what I'm trying to save. Community is my motivation for environmental choices … it's for the whole world! I don't want to just save my children's future. I want to be woven in.

Fiona is concerned with environmental justice and frames her interest in the environment in terms of a concern for the impact of her choices on other people, both locally and globally.

Fiona: I want other people to not be exposed to toxins, and especially I think in American culture there tends to be a lot of waste in resource use, and that makes me concerned about the impacts on other parts of the world. I feel like there's some environmental injustice that happens when we ship all of our garbage off to other places.

Leonda and Rebecca are motivated by concerns related to social justice and see social justice and environmental justice as linked.

Rebecca: My views on social justice are very much related to my beliefs about the environment. One of the things that has caused all of these problems with the environment is a sense of entitlement and a lack of community-mindedness.

Leonda: My social justice and environmental interests overlap. What I noticed, when I was younger, was that a lot of environmental damage happens in places that have more poverty, like the place I grew up. In 2014, there was a chemical spill in our drinking water, and it wasn't reported for a while after the fact. I was pregnant at that time, and I drank that water. It smelled and tasted weird. And what I found out later was that the chemical that was leaked

54

into our drinking water was a chemical used to clean coal. Where I grew up, there are chemical plants all over the place, but they are in the poor areas. Not up in the mountains near the people who have money. People with more money, the CEOs of the plants, they don't really care about "uneducated" poor folks who haven't been given a lot of opportunity. The people in charge see us as a nuisance.

While Rebecca's concerns about social justice are related to her work as an educator and her reading, Leonda's concerns about social and environmental justice are the result of their first-hand experience as a Black parent and the victim of an industrial chemical spill in a highly industrial low-income region of the United States.

Penny contrasts her own priorities with those of other sustainability-oriented people she knows.

Penny: A lot of people who buy organic food, it's because they're trying to avoid pesticides for themselves or their children. They're not trying to think about the impact that's having on water pollution or air pollution or anyone else's health that's working on or living near those conventional fields. Personal care products, maybe they're buying them not because those products are less impactful for the environment, but more because they believe it's better for them. Or my vegetarian friends are [vegetarian] because they care about the individual animals or they think it's healthier for themselves, but it's never about the greenhouse gasses or the pollution or the environment.

While Penny is mostly concerned with the large-scale global impacts of her choices, she criticizes other sustainability-minded households for being more worried about the impacts on their own household members than the larger community or concerned with individual abstract farm animals rather than entire ecosystems. This same contrast is evident in the way that Jim and Sarah talk about their motivations for buying organic items.

Jim: I feel like a lot of people buy organic cotton because they feel like the pesticides are a problem for their own health, but we are more interested in the environmental impacts of the growing of the cotton. Like water consumption and pesticides. I am more interested in the public health effects on the people working on the fields and the environmental effects on nonhumans.

Sarah: We try to do everything organic. We've always been big organic buyers, and that's something that I grew up with, too. I don't want to hurt things or do things that are bad for the environment. We found out about some pesticides that were sterilizing the men who were picking fruit. I wasn't as concerned about myself as I was about the workers and the effect on them, and what it means if something like that is going into the ground. It just seems like a really bad thing. That's messed up.

Penny, Jim, and Sarah see themselves as different from the people they know who are interested in sustainability because personal health is not their primary motivation for these practices and concerns.

For Kyle and Kelly, the arrangement of nuclear families into homes drives a pattern of consumption that they see as absurd and unsustainable.

Kyle: The intentional community and commune culture is appealing to me—benign tribalism where people get to have community and join forces economically, personally, and culturally. Everyone doesn't need to have their own washing machine that goes unused 95 percent of the time, or your own car, or your own house! People living in their own houses is just absurd. The consumer culture driven by the need to sell stuff for ever higher profits creates these absurdities. And you need to be intentional if you want to do something different.

The community focus of their sustainability practices extends to their decision to turn their own home into an intentional community that houses a group of people who would conventionally live in three separate dwellings. Kyle and Kelly see living in intentional community as a solution to both environmental and social problems.

Conclusion

You may have had images and assumptions about what the adults in a sustainable household with young children in Portland are like—relatively affluent, White, engaging in conspicuous green consumption, politically progressive. Perhaps what comes to mind is something like the Sacha Baron Cohen character Dr. Nira Cain-N'Degeocello from *Who is America?*; or upscale restaurant customers in *Portlandia*—dressed up in their finest ethically sourced hemp clothing and ethnic jewelry—presented with a photo and biographical dossier on Colin, the local organic chicken on the menu; or maybe some grown-up version of Neil from *The Young Ones*, raising a family after graduating from his degree in Peace Studies.

In this chapter, I have shown that these stereotypes are not accurate—there was substantial diversity among the sustainability-oriented households with young children in Portland, Oregon, with whom I spoke, in terms of their personal backgrounds, household configurations, socioeconomic status, political leanings, education, race and ethnicity, and the gender of the householders. There is also diversity among the priorities that influence the changes my informants have made in their lives compared to what they see as more conventional ways of getting things done—my informants are motivated by priorities in personal health, nature, waste avoidance, technology, and community. The combination of priorities, resources, and constraints in each of these sustainability-oriented households determines how households get things done in everyday life via easy-to-overlook routinized practices, as everyone tries to get by in a world that often seems like it is not set up to promote the well-being of their families, communities, and the environment. In Chapter 4 I will turn to a discussion of the other side of this equation—household resources and constraints.

References

Barrett, Michèle (1980) *Women's Oppression Today: Problems in Marxist Feminist Analysis*, London: Verso.

Bernstein, Arielle (2016) "Marie Kondo and the privilege of clutter," *The Atlantic*, March 25, Available: http://www.theatlantic.com/entertainm ent/archive/2016/03/marie-kondo-and-the-privilege-of-clutter/475266/ [Accessed August 19, 2016].

Bourdieu, Pierre (1984) *Distinction: A Social Critique of the Judgement of Taste*, translated by Richard Nice, Cambridge, MA: Harvard University Press.

Chayka, Kyle (2016) "The oppressive gospel of 'minimalism,'" *New York Times*, July 26, Available: http://www.nytimes.com/2016/07/31/magaz ine/the-oppressive-gospel-of-minimalism.html?_r=0 [Accessed August 19, 2016].

Collins, Jane L. (1990) "Unwaged labor in comparative perspective: Recent theories and unanswered questions," in Jane L. Collins and Martha Giménez (eds) *Work without Wages: Comparative Studies of Domestic Labor and Self-Employment*, Albany: State University of New York Press, pp 3–24.

Dunlap, Riley E. and Araon M. McCright (2008) "A widening gap: Republican and Democratic views on climate change," *Environment: Science and Policy for Sustainable Development*, 50(5): 26–35.

Foden-Vencil, Kristian (2015) "Oregon has Highest Vaccine Exemption Rate in US," *Oregon Public Broadcasting News*, February 4, Available: https:// web.archive.org/web/20160623143332/www.opb.org/news/article/ore gon-has-highest-vaccine-exemption-rate-in-us/ [Accessed May 30, 2017].

Kyrk, Hazel (1923) *A Theory of Consumption*, Boston: Houghton Mifflin Company.

Logan, Dana W. (2017) "The lean closet: Asceticism in post-industrial consumer culture," *Journal of the American Academy of Religion*, 78(1): 1–39.

Munro, Kirstin (2021) "The welfare state and the bourgeois family-household," *Science & Society*, 85(2): 199–206.

Netting, Robert, Richard R. Wilk, and Eric J. Arnould (1984) "Introduction," in Robert Netting, Richard R. Wilk, and Eric J. Arnould (eds) *Households: Comparative and Historical Studies of the Domestic Group*, Berkeley: University of California Press.

Weber, Max (2002 [1905]) *The Protestant Ethic and the "Spirit" of Capitalism and Other Writings*, translated by Peter Baehr and Gordon C. Wells, New York: Penguin Books.

4

Resources and Constraints in Eco-Conscious Households

In this chapter, I will tell you about the resources available to my informants as they go about getting things done in everyday life, as well as the factors that constrain their ability to get things done and the options available to them.

Households draw upon a variety of resources to get things done in everyday life, but these resources can be simplified to three major overlapping categories: money, time, and know-how. Money is used to buy items the household uses or transforms, pay for assistance, and to pay for education and training. Money is obtained through government assistance, trading an adult's time for wages or self-employment income, and directly (cash) or indirectly (gifts) from extended family members. Time is used to transform purchased inputs into usable final-use goods and services, to locate free or cheaper items, to obtain money through waged work, and to obtain know-how. Time can come from household adults or extended family and friends. Know-how (in other words, competence in theories of social practice or human capital in economics) includes the skills that allow household members to produce usable goods and services in the home, to trade their time for a higher-than-subsistence wage, and to find and understand information about sustainability practices. Obtaining know-how requires time, and in some cases money.

However, these resources are not limitless. In particular, households describe making decisions on a foundation of limited time and limited money, with time constraints by far the most common concern of my informants. Households are also constrained by social and cultural norms, particularly around cleanliness. Finally, information about sustainability and sustainability practices can be difficult to find, and in some cases accurate information is not available.

Household resources

Resources from waged work

Every household I spoke with had at least one adult who engaged in waged work or self-employment for money, and both adults worked for money in nearly all of the households with two adults. Heather decided on a career as a nurse because she knew the schedule would be compatible with her desire be available for her children during the day, and Emily's hours as a consultant are flexible and have allowed her to adjust her schedule to accommodate childcare obligations during her children's different life stages. Ian is a self-employed artist who is responsible for much of the household's childcare needs, Scott's work flexibility allows him to be home when Sarah travels for work, and Jim spent time at home while Jess worked when their child was a baby. Overall, however, women were more likely to have flexible jobs for childcare purposes or to not work outside the home. Penny worked part-time while her children were young and she was married. Since her recent divorce, she would like to work more, but her employer so far hasn't been willing to increase her hours. However, Orla has been working between 50–60 hours fairly consistently, a schedule that she finds challenging.

While Emily, Gloria's husband, and Sarah telecommute, most of my informants do travel to jobs with worksites outside the home, which takes additional time. Quinn's bus commute is close to an hour and a half each way, though she will also take the bus to work and then ride her bike home when the weather is nice out. Jess used to commute by car to a job around 90 minutes away, but she is happier now that she can ride her bike to work in downtown Portland, just a few miles away. Informants told me that they appreciate having jobs that allow them to bike commute or take public transportation, with on-site showers making the bike commute more feasible during hot summer months. The lack of employer-provided parking in downtown Portland also contributes to the decision to get to work by bus or bike, as does the fact that rush-hour traffic often means that driving a car to work will take longer than bus or bike. For other informants, a lack of time contributes to their need to drive to work.

Many of the informants in this study have jobs at least tangentially related to their sustainability interests. There are several possible explanations for this. First, people who have a strong interest in sustainability may feel that it is important for their choice of paid employment to also be an expression of these values. Second, Portland is a city with a large number of these kinds of "green" jobs. Third, consistent with Chiswick (1999) and Chiswick and Chiswick (2000), there may be feedback loops between sustainability practices inside the home and sustainability employment outside the home. It may be the case that employment-specific sustainability human capital that one acquires in college, for example in an environmental sciences degree, or on the job, for example as an energy-efficiency consultant, also makes it easier to engage in sustainability practices in the home, for example by decreasing the amount of work required to find out about recycling sorting or energy-efficiency rebates. The reverse may also be true. The domestic-specific human capital acquired on the job as a sustainability-oriented parent may also have some usefulness for certain paid jobs—such a feedback loop influenced Fiona's career as a preschool teacher and Heather's work as a doula. Kelly began working as a midwife prior to becoming a parent, and struggles with this career choice. She has been pondering switching to another career that is more consistent with her overall values of service, community, and social justice because she is concerned her current work doesn't meet an "unmet need" in Portland. There were very few people I spoke with who had completely "conventional" corporate careers—having a job that is consistent with their values is important to my informants.

Resources from extended family and friends

Two of the households I spoke with had grandparents who were living in the household at least part of the time to provide extra help getting things done. Amy's father has been living in their home part of the time to help Amy and Andrew cope with their busy jobs.

Andrew: Amy's father has been living with us a bit, sort of on and off to help with kids as we're juggling our schedules.

Kelly's mother moved into her home to help her and Kyle with childcare, and Kelly's mother now also runs a preschool business out of the home. Prior to having their second child, Mike and Mina relocated to Portland from another state to be closer to Mina's parents and extended family. Eric and Emily relocated to be closer to Eric's parents hoping to get additional support and assistance with their children, but returned to Portland when they weren't getting the type of help they had wanted. Grandparents also help by buying things for the household, even if they aren't present living in the household, as Amy and Andrew, Fiona, and Eric and Emily reported. This kind of help can sometimes be a problem for sustainability-oriented families when grandparents have different priorities and don't understand what is wanted or needed and why.

Other friends, neighbors, and community members also provide help. Sometimes this help is paid, such as the neighbor that Eric and Emily pay to watch their son on days he is not in daycare. Sometimes this help is based on reciprocity, like carpooling, the childcare agreements in a cohousing community, or shared food and meals in an intentional community. Bike advocates Victor and Vanessa take advantage of carpooling to get their children to out-of-town soccer games. They also rely on their neighbors in their cohousing community to keep an eye on their children when they leave the children alone. Kyle and Kelly share childcare tasks and meals with the other family living in their home in intentional community. Gloria does not have close connections with her biological family, but she values the reciprocity of sharing resources in her community.

Gloria: Receiving help and offering help are vital for us.

Other informants de-emphasized the importance of help in their lives, priding themselves on self-reliance and independence as expressions of their sustainability values.

Dayna: I'd say self-sufficiency or self-reliance is something that is a theme for a lot of the decisions that we make.

Dayna: Gardening ties back to an aspect of self-sufficiency for me. And I just like it? It brings me a lot of satisfaction. I get a similar sense of satisfaction from growing my own electricity as growing my own food. I *can*! It is something that is achievable and is something that I can do. And it makes me feel good.

However, there were ironies involved. For example, David and Dayna purchased a dilapidated home, which they renovated extensively with the help of Dayna's father, a retired general contractor who supplied the tools and four months of his free labor. They would not have been able to afford to buy a habitable home. Buying a house that was "condemned" and fixing it up made home ownership possible. Similarly, they "grow their own" electricity with government-subsidized solar panels.

Resources from government and nonprofits

Households also employ resources from government programs and nonprofit organizations, though the redistributive nature of these programs was not highlighted by informants who benefited from them. Leonda told me about receiving Temporary Assistance for Needy Families (TANF), food benefits, and Special Supplemental Nutrition for Women, Infants, and Children (WIC).

Leonda: It's a generational kind of thing. My grandmother had benefits, and then my mom had it, and then when I got pregnant my grandmother told me I needed to go get benefits.

Leonda also visits food banks to get extra food for their family. It is likely that, based on their incomes, more of my informants receive food benefits, Medicaid, and other government transfer payments, but they did not discuss these programs with me, and I did not ask any direct questions about government benefits. Fiona told me about participating in a low-income program that gave her a free set of cloth diapers on a rental basis. When she received her tax refund, presumably including state and federal Earned Income Tax Credits, she returned the rental diapers and purchased her own set of secondhand cloth diapers.

Other redistributive programs accessed by my informants are not targeted toward low-income households and may in fact regressively transfer wealth from low-income households to moderate- and high-income households. Eric and Emily and Owen and Orla had made energy-efficiency improvements to their homes that were subsidized, paid for out of the public purpose charge for all Oregon utility ratepayers with additional tax deductions in some cases. In addition to other subsidized energy-efficiency improvements, Chris and Carrie, David and Dayna, and Kyle and Kelly have solar panels on their homes. While Chris and Carrie seemed ambivalent about their solar panels and Kyle was vocally skeptical of them, Dayna was an enthusiastic advocate for residential solar power. The net metering electricity tariff in Oregon at the time the research was conducted is designed such that Dayna's family pays only a monthly connection fee. Dayna's household generates more electricity than it uses each year, and the utility is required to credit the household for their excess generation at the retail rate. This means at night and during the peak electricity demand hours when their solar panels are not generating electricity, Dayna's household cashes in their electricity credits. In addition to the subsidy to their monthly bills, the households with solar panels also received a combination of subsidies for the installation of the panels, including subsidies paid for by the public purpose charge and state and federal tax credits. David and Dayna report that their savings in electricity costs over the past eight years have more than made up for the up-front costs of buying and installing their solar system. Ironically, these solar panels, which were effectively paid for by the government and other utility rate-payers, represent independence, self-sufficiency, and a lack of reliance on the electric utility for David and Dayna.

Dayna: I like that I feel that we are self-sufficient. The self-sufficiency aspect. The same way that it makes me feel good to be able to grow a portion of our own food. To be able to be generating our own electricity, that makes me feel really good. It's just damn satisfying, too. Our system produces 100 percent of our electricity on an annual basis. And it is so satisfying every March to get our net excess generation letter from

	PGE [Portland General Electric, an electricity utility] where they're like "you had excess generation credit because your system produced more electricity than you used in a year."
David:	And as long as our solar electric system is on the roof, that will always be the case unless something happens to net metering. That's pretty great because we prepurchased our electricity for the foreseeable future and we never have to worry about that expense ever again. And the up-front investment I think is essentially paid off now.
Kirstin:	So, you think it's paid for itself through the lower electricity costs?
Dayna:	Yeah, the combination of the incentives and tax credits that we got. Those rolled in within the first four years of the system.

Of course, our conversation took place after dark, and their home was lighted—presumably with electricity from the grid.

Brian, Victor and Vanessa, and Yvonne send their children to sustainability-oriented public schools. Victor and Vanessa like the fact that their children's school reflects the values and priorities of their family with school policies like requiring children not be allowed any "screen time" during the week at home. Heather and Gloria, however, homeschool their children because they believe that public schools don't adequately reflect the values and priorities of their families. Brian acknowledges that these special schools are somewhat controversial, as not everyone has the money needed to afford to buy or rent property near the school his child attends, but he is happy that his child is receiving a high-quality free education. The remainder of the households I spoke with were sending their school-aged children to their neighborhood public school. Other than daycares and preschools, none of the households I spoke with were sending their children to private schools.

Public transportation and cycling infrastructure like bike lanes and off-street bike paths provided by the city are another way my informants' sustainability practices benefit from government-provided resources. While not ubiquitous, biking and taking public transportation were the most common ways the informants got to their jobs.

| Fiona: | The bus is so easy and quick here. In Central Oregon, it doesn't run past 6 pm or on Sunday which is absurd! So, bigger towns and bigger cities, the transit system really makes a huge impact. |
| Andrew: | Being in a place like Portland where infrastructure exists and culture exists where these things are encouraged and made easier ... not everything is easy, but, you know where it is easier to do things ... That for me is key. |

The availability of these government resources reduces the costs of car-free commutes and makes it easier to get around in a way that is consistent with my informants' priorities.

Resources from research

My informants told me that they feel fortunate to be able to do research into sustainability practices, to understand this research, and to have the types of educations that allow them to access these types of information. Research allows my respondents to become more efficient at their sustainability practices, to learn new ways of doing things that are consistent with their priorities, and find out information about the potential impacts of their practices. A more detailed discussion of household research, the factors that motivate this research, and the social meanings of this research, as well as its limitations, appears in Chapter 7.

Resources from gleaning, borrowed and free items, and theft

While many of my informants try to reduce their overall waste by giving away unwanted items for free to friends or through online groups, other informants actively engage in provisioning for their families through "gleaning"—meaning obtaining items for free that other people no longer want. Vanessa says she "can't resist a good free box," meaning items left on the sidewalk for people to pick through and take what they want. Similarly, Ian says he probably takes things home that he finds in sidewalk free boxes more than would be ideal, and his wife agrees.

Ian: I don't really like buying new things. I do a good amount of free boxing. Probably more than I should, I'll pick something up.

Ivy: Oh great, more shit! Look at our house! It is insane in here!

The interior of Ian and Ivy's colorful and artistic home was cluttered, filled with piles of clothing left over from a recent "naked lady" used-clothing swap party and other random items. While Ian doesn't mind the untidiness, Ivy finds it stressful. When their household relocated to Oregon, Leonda was able to get most of their furniture for free from coworkers and online free groups. Orla points out that obtaining things her household needs for free takes additional time that a working family with children can't always devote to this type of "scavenging."

Orla: Since becoming a parent, I do much less scavenging for free stuff. You have to search and you have to have the flexibility to go and get stuff right when you see it. I would like to do more of that.

She believes her friends without children are much more successful at gleaning than she is able to be, and she looks forward to getting back to doing more gleaning when she has more time. Gloria told me that her husband is much more willing to spend time getting items they need second hand or for free—Gloria is much more likely to prefer the less time-consuming route, while her husband has a high tolerance for spending time hunting for the things they need for cheap or free.

Gleaning and free boxes were not the only ways that my informants got things without paying for them—Leonda told me about stealing organic and other expensive health food items from grocery stores.

Leonda: I don't put my produce in plastic bags except for apples. And I'm not going to tell you why because it's illegal! [laughing] I put a different number in at the self-checkout because the Gala apples are always on sale, so I put the more expensive organic apples in the bag, and tie it up and call it Galas. I do it with dried mangoes, too. I call that bananas.

Their friends who have worked in grocery stores taught them how to use the wrong bulk bin codes at the self-checkout. They do this because they feel they can't afford to buy the items they want on their budget, even with food stamps.

Resources from unwaged work

Only three of the adults in this study do not work for money outside the home—Gloria, Mina, and Vanessa. These informants and their households see their unwaged work as a direct substitute for waged work and the goods and services that they would need to pay for if these women were working outside the home.

Mina: I'm a stay-at-home mom and my time is my value to the household.
Victor: There are some major savings associated with having Vanessa stay home: childcare, less convenience meals out, fewer vehicle expenses, less income taxes. And there is almost just as large a number of small savings which one has to be plugged into the "alt-mom" community to know about. Being able to put time and effort into tracking sales, pacing purchases, and planning where and when you shop to get the best discounts can make for huge savings. I don't keep close track anymore, but our grocery spend for a family of five is about $1,000–1,200/month. Fifteen years ago, when

it was just me and Vanessa, we probably spent $800–900 a month. The difference then is that we both worked full-time. If Vanessa went back to working full-time, I bet our grocery bill would go up 50 percent. There's also a lot less self-medicating with junk food, "nights out," and fancy vacations when one's not stressed from being overscheduled all the time.

But this is not to say they aren't working outside the home, they just aren't being paid for this work. Both Mina and Vanessa engage in considerable unwaged work outside the home in their children's schools, and Vanessa does the laundry at her church on a volunteer basis. Gloria prides herself on giving back to her community, and her connections to community are her primary motivation for her sustainability practices. She also homeschools her four children, a decision she made in order to remove her children from what she believes is a disrespectful culture that is excessively focused on consumerism.

Yvonne works around 15 hours a week for her husband's landscaping business, but she sees herself as a stay-at-home mother and views her work on their urban homestead as contributing to the household in a way that substitutes for paid employment.

Yvonne: I used to work full-time. I had two jobs—I was a bartender and worked in a restaurant. We were a double-income family like most families probably are. When I was seven months pregnant with my third child, we decided as a family that the trade-off for me not working would be me doing all of the homesteading-type things. If both parents are working full-time, it is just too hard to do the amount of work that is required for homesteading, to be that sustainable. We decided that if we want this to be our lifestyle, then I need to be here full-time. This is my job—to make up for my lack of income through all of the other ways I help us save money.

While Heather works more than full-time between her waged job and self-employment ventures, her overnight weekend work as a nurse enables her to act as a stay-at-home mother and homeschool her three children during the week. Having been raised by an unreliable single mother, being present for her own children and involved in their lives is an important priority for Heather.

Of course, unwaged work in households is not limited to women who are stay-at-home mothers or whose waged work schedules allow them to act as stay-at-home mothers. Informants whose households have two adults who work full-time on conventional schedules also get things done using their time and effort, and an interest in sustainability often means additional tasks or more time-consuming ones. Tasks like healthcare, childcare, food preparation, home repairs, transportation, shopping, and cleaning—most of the tasks in everyday life—are chores that my informants could pay someone else to do or that the government could provide on a collective basis, but that they do themselves instead.

Many informants venerate the idea of doing things themselves, particularly in the realms of intensive food preparation and home improvements. Home-cooked meals from scratch were particularly important to many informants. During our conversation, Kelly shared some delicious homemade seaweed crackers with me—because of her flexible work schedule, she winds up doing more than half of the food preparation in their immediate family, though the four other adults living in her home also share the burden. Chris says that most of the food his family eats is cooked from scratch except crackers and English muffins, though he bakes all of the family's bread and makes elaborate meals. A combination of personal interest, ability, and work schedules drives Leonda, Jim, Owen, Nathan, Rebecca, and Tim to be the primary evening meal cooks in their households, and the remaining households with two working adults told me that this chore is shared about evenly.

Home improvement tasks, on the other hand, were largely a male enterprise. Heather and Gloria's husbands built their chicken coops, and Heather describes a division of labor in their home in which her husband, who is a professional carpenter, is responsible for things on the "outside" of the home, while Heather, a nurse, is responsible for tasks on the "inside" of the home.

Heather: He does most of the work with the chickens. He built the chicken coop, he does most of the cleaning of it. He puts them out and lets them in every day. Outside is him. But inside the house, it's flip-flopped. When it comes to caring for the kids, making the medical decisions, making the nutritional decisions.

Andrew and Amy recently moved into an older home, and Andrew has been spending time on repairs and renovations. Kyle and David and Dayna point to the "sweat equity" that they invested in their homes, the extensive renovations of which would not have been possible without the unwaged work done by themselves and others.

Informants who were not able to engage in some of these more intensive practices, relying instead on purchased inputs, frequently expressed feelings of guilt or inadequacy. While Fiona does cook nightly meals for herself and her children, she wishes she were doing more intensive scratch cooking from dry ingredients and whole foods rather than relying on what she sees as "convenience items" like canned beans. David and Dayna and Quinn's families eat a lot of frozen convenience foods, which saves time.

Quinn: If I had more time, I would eat less packaged food and less convenience food.

Fiona: With working and coming home so late on the bus, it is less frequent that I make meals that are just bulk grains and beans and things like that. So that's still kind of a goal, but it doesn't happen as much.

Informants frequently told me that they would do more intensive cooking if they had more time to engage in this work.

 Heather, Gloria, Ivy, and Mina all spoke longingly of the idea of homesteading, or self-sufficient subsistence home farming and provisioning involving large expenditures of unwaged time and few purchased inputs. They see this living arrangement of intensive home production as a perfect embodiment of sustainable living.

Ivy: When I think about homesteading, I feel like my whole body would thank me and my spirit would calm. I feel like I would be a healthier, happier person because I wouldn't be like rushing around, going to work, doing this, you know? There is just something so calming and healthy about the homesteading life. You have a lot of work to do, but it is all great for your body and you're doing it for the people around you.

Homesteading is thought of favorably by many—but not all—of my informants. Rebecca and Kyle weren't interested in homesteading as a sustainability practice, Rebecca because she didn't feel that she would enjoy the homesteading lifestyle and Kyle because he is skeptical that it is a more environmental choice.

Rebecca: My brother and sister-in-law have two kids, and they grow all of their own food, they reuse a lot of things, they make their own yogurt, they do a lot of sewing, and his business is around using salvaged wood. They do it very cheaply because they have a stay-at-home parent and more of a homestead thing. They are substituting time for money.

Rebecca explicitly highlights the substitutability of unwaged work spent in household production and commodities purchased with money from waged work that I discuss in Chapter 2. Similarly, Jim would prefer to live in a homesteading-style situation in a rural area, but he believes this is a less environmental option than living in an urban area. However, for many of the sustainability-oriented households I spoke with, it seems that the ideal would be to rely to the greatest extent possible on unwaged work in the home and as little as possible on purchased inputs and government resources. Yvonne, whose household comes closest to this homesteading ideal of anyone I spoke with for this book, ultimately found the amount of unwaged work involved unmanageable, and had to give up raising livestock to maintain her "sanity."

Household constraints

The resources available to households to get things done in everyday life are not present in infinite quantities. The constraints experienced by my informants may be related to the organization of the economy and society in capitalism, they may be related to cultural and social conventions, or they may be related to path-dependent factors in the lives of individuals—though these sources of constraint are recursively related. There is nothing that forces my informants to work long hours at their paid jobs, limiting the time they have available for other activities. However, they may feel very much compelled to work these hours for a variety of reasons—a desire to provide a certain level of consumption for their families that is achieved in this society through waged work, a feeling of investment in the mission of their employer, or because these extended hours have become the convention for full-time workers. On the other side of this same coin, the budgets of some informants are limited because no full-time work is available. They are compelled by the organization of capitalist society to at least partially meet their day-to-day needs with money. There is nothing that requires children be raised by their parents in households, but this is the convention in the culture and society in which we live, and this type of time-intensive childcare provided by family members limits the time available to adults for other activities. There is nothing that forces anyone to take a particular job (whether waged or unwaged), but the path toward this occupation likely began decades prior, limited by initial conditions and with potential options narrowing with each passing year. Constraints, both external and ones that may appear to be self-imposed, place real limits on my informants' choices.

Time constraints

A concern about lack of time was expressed in almost every conversation with informants for this study. Families find it difficult to cope with the burdens of their waged jobs, the unwaged work of everyday life as a parent, and the frequently time-consuming sustainability practices they've undertaken. Even stay-at-home mothers felt pressed for time as they juggled the many obligations of an intensive and professionalized mothering métier. An editorial from over sixty years ago rings true today: "When millions of workers are expressing the same gripe about their job … it is no longer a gripe, it becomes a social problem. That gripe or grievance no longer affects just this or that individual, it affects all of society" ("Gripes and Grievances" 1955, 4). My informants told me that they often feel exhausted and depleted. They make trade-offs to cope with life's demands, but they are not happy about having to make these compromises. There is simply not enough time in the day to get everything done.

Several informants told me in general terms that they didn't have enough time, linking this reality to the demands of work and parenting young children.

Emily: I think Eric would agree with the assessment that the thing we are most short on is free time.

Andrew: I feel like for me it's a balancing act. You know, I have all of these things that I'm dealing with on a daily basis, with kids, and job, and whatever, right? I have really limited bandwidth at this point in my life. I feel like time is becoming more and more valuable, because I feel like I don't have enough of it, right?

Emily and Andrew's households both attempted to alleviate the time-intensive parenting burdens by relying on help from grandparents, with mixed success.

After long days of work, my informants were exhausted and find that they lack the time and energy to get everyday tasks done, like buying groceries and basic meal preparation.

Sarah: We order the groceries online for delivery from a local store pretty regularly. We are just so tired, and then if one of us goes out to get the groceries, then the other is stuck here with the kids.

Quinn: We eat a lot of processed foods, a lot of microwaved foods. A lot of Amy's [vegetarian brand frozen meals]. We're working and then getting home, and we're just tired.

Sarah and Quinn wind up substituting market goods and services—delivery service and frozen convenience foods—for more time-intensive ways of getting shopping and meal preparation done.

Other informants told me that they often lack time for time-intensive sustainability practices, so they wind up relying on what they view as less sustainable or less healthy ways of getting things done.

Leonda: I am lazy, that's my only real reason for not making my own laundry detergent and dish soap. I could totally make that stuff, but it is very time-consuming and seems like a daunting task when I already have so much else to do.

Orla: If we had more time, we wouldn't have to buy so much packaged snack food for the kids. We go through a lot of apple sauce pouches. We recycle them, but it would be nice to not buy them in the first place. I don't have time to refill reusable pouches, and I don't want to do the dishes associated.

Amy: If I had more time, I would want to make the kids' snacks and stuff more versus just buying the packaged stuff. But that's something that I don't have time for, so it doesn't happen.

Chris: No, but the other piece of it [commuting by bike less frequently] was just the time biking back home was starting to feel like more of a crunch. And my job just got more stressful over a little while during that time. And I was needing to stay later, so just the sheer time was an impediment.

Time-intensive sustainability practices get put on the back burner when other stresses of everyday life take a priority, but my informants rarely feel good about these compromises.

Budget constraints

None of my informants emphasized feeling financially constrained, including those of my informants who reported the lowest incomes. Perhaps financial resources are in many cases the flip side of time constraints, though this is not always the case. The low-income households I spoke with also reported feeling significantly pressed for time. Even Penny, a single mother who works part-time and has two school-aged children who live with her half of the time, felt far more constrained by her schedule than by her budget. To some extent, an interest in the sustainability realm means that these households are generally aware of and engaging in sustainability practices that also save money, for example, turning down the heat and not using much space cooling, cloth diapering, reducing their overall consumption, vegetable gardening and putting food by, owning fewer vehicles (if any), and obtaining needed items for free or secondhand.

My informants did share with me some ways that they maintain their sustainability practices on their budgets. Emily, Mina, and Vanessa make over four grocery store trips per week to a variety of stores to buy the items their households need at the specific stores where these items are the cheapest. Households rarely told me that they buy exclusively organic food items, instead prioritizing the "Dirty Dozen" list of products that have the highest amount of pesticide and other chemical residues. Jim and Wendy told me about being unhappy with occasionally buying children's clothes at big-box stores like Target rather than secondhand or boutique organic items that would be unaffordable for a fast-growing toddler.

When I asked my informants if they believed living in a sustainable way was more expensive than a conventional lifestyle, the answer I heard most frequently was some variation of "Not if you're doing it right."

Gloria: It seems expensive, because maybe the bottle of sustainable shampoo is so much more expensive than a conventional bottle. But you're taking a shorter shower, and you're using towels that you've had for ten years because you don't buy new ones every three years when you also repaint all the walls. Item by item, these things can be far more expensive. But the lifestyle is incredibly economical.

Penny: If you want to grow your own food that will be the most sustainable and also the cheapest. Or you can buy that food, and it is going to be expensive.

While certain aspects of a sustainability-oriented way of getting things done may be more expensive, like out-of-season organic produce or other specialty items, my informants generally believe that a truly sustainable household wouldn't be buying things like that in the first place. An exception to this was renters in my sample, Fiona and Tim and Tara, who talked about their incomes preventing them from buying their own homes. They believe home ownership would allow them to make more drastic sustainability lifestyle choices, such as intensive vegetable gardening, raising home livestock, and installing solar panels.

Social and cultural constraints

My informants have made changes to conventional ways of getting things done, but they often remain constrained in their ability to make changes because of a desire to life in a way that is compatible with the wider culture and social understandings of the boundaries of acceptable behavior. Penny is an environmental educator, and as a result of her training and career she was one of my most ecologically aware informants. At the same time, she was very honest and pragmatic about her life and the trade-offs involved in her practices. When I spoke with her, she was dressed smartly in a fashionable athletic zip-up jacket with a jaunty and trendy asymmetrical collar.

Penny: If you really wanted to be as sustainable as possible, you would never buy any new clothes or get everything out of free boxes. You could stay dressed for free, but you might not look very stylish ... In the perfect world, you could not consume anything and be OK with it. But in reality, we live in a society where there are other pressures and we don't have as much time as it would take to live in a way that would be nice to live.

Heather told me about wanting to make sure her children were able to integrate into the mainstream culture, unlike some "wild and free" families she knows who live more extreme rural homesteading lifestyles.

Heather: We have friends who are like constantly naked outside. Which is fine ... And I can appreciate why they do that, but I feel like we need some balance to be able to function in our society.

There are limits to how far my informants are willing to go outside the bounds of culturally acceptable behavior for their sustainability practices. To some extent, living in a place with a lot of like-minded people means being surrounded by a different cultural mindset than if my informants lived in a more conventional place, or a place with more people who are hostile to environmental concerns. Victor, Vanessa, David, Dayna, Eric, and Brian all expressed a feeling that their reliance on bicycles for transportation is largely enabled by Portland's "bike culture" and acceptance of cycling as a valid way for adults to get to work. The lack of social acceptance of cycling in other regions may limit the abilities of adults in those places to bike commute, both indirectly through raised eyebrows or a lack of awareness of cycling as an option, or more directly through a lack of the infrastructures that help enable cycling like workplace showers and bike lanes. However, not everything about a sustainability-oriented local culture is necessarily a good thing. Mina spoke to me in hushed tones when she told me that all of her children are fully vaccinated, and that they received those vaccinations on the conventional schedule. She believes that the other parents at her preschool, where a large proportion of the children are unvaccinated, would judge her harshly for vaccinating her children.

Cultural expectations for comfort and cleanliness also place constraints on the ways that my informants get things done, as will be discussed in more detail in Chapter 6. Many mundane, taken-for-granted everyday things in our lives are the product of culture: what a clean bathroom looks like and how it gets that way, how often a person should shower, what the inside of a home should feel like in hot weather and cold weather, what clothing should smell like, where to store eggs. One particular subject stood out as having particular cultural significance for my informants: what a clean bathroom towel should feel like.

Jim: We use the dryer as little as possible. Almost never. Towels and sheets we line dry, and guests complain about them for sure.

Because tumble dryers are relatively ubiquitous in U.S. single-family homes, most of my informants grew up with towels that were washed in a conventional washing machine and dried in a tumble dryer. Chris and Wendy were the exceptions. Wendy grew up in South America with line-dried towels, and she loves the feeling of towels fresh off the line. For Wendy, soft towels that were dried in a tumble-dryer feel dirty and don't smell right. Chris had countercultural ecologically oriented parents who line-dried all of their laundry, and when he went to college he learned to love the feeling of soft, tumble-dried laundry.

Chris: Yeah, the dryer I've always loved. It was a total guilty pleasure when I went to college and I didn't have to hang up my clothes anymore! I remember that.

While Heather grew up with tumble-dried towels, she lived for a few years in England as an adult and hated the crunchy line-dried laundry. Other than Wendy and Jim and Jess, towels are an item that must be dried in the tumble dryer for my informants who line-dry their clothes.

Penny: When it's warm, I hang out my laundry in the backyard. I don't like when towels are hung out to dry because they aren't soft. So sometimes I will hang them out to dry, and then finish them off in the dryer to fluff them up.

David: We just sort of started doing it because we were cognizant of the amount of energy a dryer uses. So, when the weather is nice we opt to hang it up.

Dayna: It is better. Everything except for towels. Towels do better in the dryer.

David: That's true. They get so scratchy when they're sun-dried.

Cultural expectations for cleanliness and comfort shape the way my informants get things done, and they have grown accustomed to towels that feel and smell a certain way. While some of my informants have made a major intervention into a conventional way of getting things done in the United States by line-drying their laundry, the culture they live in has taught them that towels should be soft and fluffy. Cultural and social norms place limits on how far my informants are willing to go for their sustainability practices.

Information constraints

My informants divert time away from other priorities and everyday tasks to research their practices and consumption decisions, but there are limits to the available information. Emily told me that she believes it is harder for people who don't have exposure to sustainability ideas or the type of education she received to understand the research she seeks out for her family. Many informants were discouraged by contradictory information and difficulties finding good information about sustainability practices. Jim and Victor expressed the most frustration with the lack of comprehensive, accurate research on sustainability and personal health. They want to know the best ways to get things done to protect the environment and their families, but find that conclusive evidence and solid, unambiguous advice rarely exists. Victor attempts to solve this problem by conducting his own medical experiments on his family, for example by testing the efficacy of different dietary supplement regimes, but that is not the same as definitive health research. Jim searches for good information to help him make the best environmental choices, but finds it is rarely available.

Jim: I find it frustrating that I can't find information that I trust. A lot of the decisions or nondecisions that we make are because we just don't know what the right thing to do is.

He wishes he could find information about the precise relative carbon impacts of all of his choices, for example whether or not it is a good environmental choice to replace his old car with a more fuel-efficient one. Jim becomes upset at the futility of his attempts to make the best environmental choices, a feeling that becomes acute when he believes, in hindsight, that he made the wrong choice because of bad or inaccurate information.

Conclusion

If the household is like a factory that produces everyday life, the resources described in this chapter—in the forms of money from waged work, resources from extended family and friends, government assistance, know-how and research, free and gleaned items, and unwaged work—are the inputs into that household production processes. The proportions in which these inputs in routinized daily activities are used are different for each household—households have different resources available to them, but they also face different constraints in terms of information, social and cultural norms about correct ways to get things done, financial budgets, and time. A lack of time was a nearly universal concern among my informants. They find themselves exhausted by all of the competing demands in their busy lives as parents of young children, trying to balance priorities while taking on additional sometimes very time-consuming tasks related to their values in the sustainability realm.

Robbins (2007 [1932], 15) writes that "the economist studies the disposal of scarce means." However, a full understanding of social conditions requires also understanding the underlying sources of scarcity and constraints. Prior to Robbins' (2007 [1932], 4) popularization of the scarcity definition of economics, the common description of economics was as "a study of the causes of material welfare." Robbins (2007 [1932], 14) is, of course, correct in pointing out that "There are only twenty-four hours in the day. We have to choose between the different uses to which they may be put." However, in capitalism the range of options is restricted before the choosing can begin.

The precise ways that these sustainability-oriented households take care of their everyday tasks varies based on their individual combination of priorities, resources, and constraints. The households I spoke with differ in their sustainability priorities, and these differences in emphasis impact what areas of everyday life my informants have made changes to, and how they go about implementing those changes. Households also vary in terms of the amount of money they earn through waged employment, their access to help from friends and family, their knowledge from research or schooling, the resources they receive from the government and nonprofits, and how much time they have available for household tasks. Finally, these households diverge in the extent to which they are constrained by time, budgets, social and cultural concerns, and a lack of information.

Nathan and Nicole have high wage incomes and work long hours, so they can afford to have a personal assistant who takes care of home maintenance, babysits, and does their recycling and bottle return for them. They also have a housekeeper who cleans their home and helps with laundry. Since technology and avoiding waste are their sustainability priorities, they have spent a lot of money on a geothermal heat pump system and insulating their home. Eric and Emily are both white-collar professionals, and they stretched their household budget to afford a home in a neighborhood that will allow their children to walk to school from elementary school through high school. Eric bikes to work, and Emily telecommutes. Because personal health is a household priority, Emily goes to various grocery stores by car at least four times a week so that she can purchase their family health food staples at the best possible prices. Penny is a single mother of two who works part-time as an environmental educator but wishes she could work full-time. Recently, her furnace broke and she figured out how to repair it herself by watching instructional videos online. She makes special reusable toilet paper for her family out of old flannel sheets. Because she is most concerned about the impacts of her consumption choices on other people and the natural environment, she decided to commit to buying nothing other than food and fuel for the first six months of 2017.

In Chapters 5 and 6, I will describe how these differences in resources, constraints, and priorities contribute to diverse outcomes in the ways that my informants remove waste from their households, achieve cleanliness, and stay comfortable indoors. As part of this account, I will consider the changing social and cultural meanings of waste, cleanliness, and comfort for these households.

References

Chiswick, Carmel U. (1999) "The economics of Jewish continuity," *Contemporary Jewry*, 20(1): 30–56.

Chiswick, Carmel U. and Barry R. Chiswick (2000) "The cost of living Jewishly and Jewish continuity," *Contemporary Jewry*, 21(1): 78–90.

"Gripes and Grievances," (1955) *Correspondence*, 2(2): 4. Cited in Haider, Asad and Salar Mohandesi. (2013) "Workers' Inquiry: A Genealogy." *Viewpoint Magazine*, September 27, 2013. Available: https://www.viewpointmag. com/2013/09/27/workers-inquiry-a-genealogy/

Robbins, Lionel (2007) *An Essay on the Nature and Significance of Economic Science*, Auburn, AL: Mises Institute.

5

Managing Household Waste

In Chapters 3 and 4, I described my sample of eco-conscious households and the priorities, resources, and constraints that influence how they get things done in everyday life. In this chapter and Chapter 6, I will describe how these elements combine to generate a set of human activities in households that constitute everyday life. In trying to learn about how households get things done, I focused my conversations with informants on their practices with respect to six categories of daily life: waste, comfort, cleanliness, food, transportation, childcare, and general provisioning. The discussion in this book focuses on waste, indoor comfort, and cleanliness, since these are aspects of everyday life that have not received extensive attention elsewhere. Because of my interest in how practices change or are resistant to change, I asked follow-up questions to help me understand how my informants learned these practices, how these differ from the way they themselves grew up, how things have changed since becoming a parent, and what they would do differently if they had more time or money. This chapter describes how my informants deal with household solid waste.

Household waste includes trash and "packaging," compost, recycling, diapers, and toilet waste. The eco-conscious households I spoke with were almost universally concerned with reducing their consumption, and for many, the waste generated by their lifestyles and practices serves as an uncomfortable reminder of their shortcomings in the sustainability realm. For some households, practices that prevented waste from going to a landfill, such as composting and recycling, are sufficient to alleviate the guilt associated with waste-generating consumption. Other households attempt to purchase items with as little packaging as possible because recycling and composting are not enough for them to feel absolved. Waste is visible, tangible evidence of things you consumed. Once every week or two, your neighbors can see all of your trash awaiting removal right in front of your home. It smells, it is unsightly, it attracts vermin, and it triggers disgust through our instinctive drive to avoid risks of contamination, parasites, and disease (Kelly 2011, 1–58). In this sample of households, the topic of packaging—things like plastic films and cardboard boxes—elicited powerful and unexpected reactions from my informants, while practices that involve allowing organic matter to decompose in the backyard or leaving urine in a toilet bowl unflushed elicited few negative reactions. Weinbaum and Bridges (1976) point out that the work involved in consumption is the "other side of the paycheck." For these eco-conscious households, practices involving the disposal of household waste are the *other* side of the other side of the paycheck—the final phase of the consumption they wish they could avoid.

Trash and "packaging"

My informants think about trash in ways that are linked to the anti-littering public service announcement campaigns and images of swelling landfills of their childhoods (Shabecoff 1987; Cialdini 2001).

Ian: I remember in junior high them telling us not to trash the environment. And they had someone come to school in a costume dressed as a trash heap to teach us about the environment.

Owen: Growing up in the Midwest in the 1970s, people didn't talk about recycling or the environment. Our consideration of the environment was the TV commercial with a Native American guy crying because a White guy threw a beer can out the window. "Don't Litter" was it. There just wasn't a movement going on where I lived.

Tim: When I was a kid, the crying Indian ad was really big. And I remember there was a joke at the end of a Steve Martin record, where he says, "You know, it's really important if you can keep a litter bag in your car. It doesn't take up too much space. And when it's full you can throw the whole littler bag out the window." That's how he ended his whole set! That is so of that moment. That was the whole point of the crying Indian ad. Have a litter bag in your car instead of throwing it out the window.

Eric: For whatever reason, whenever I think of sustainability, or when I first realized that I had some kind of impact, was cutting the six-pack rings. Seeing a picture of one around a bird's neck, and realizing that I should cut all of those up. That was something that someone suggested to me, and so I was adamant that we should do that. And I would cut them into the smallest pieces in the world.

Trash is an evocative symbol of human impacts on the natural environment. The image of an Italian American dressed up as a Native American shedding a tear over litter and pollution (Aleiss 1999) stuck in the minds of my informants, even if they cite the "Keep America Beautiful" public service announcement campaign with an eye roll. During the 1970s and 1980s, concerns about landfills and the negative impacts of litter formed the basis of much of popular environmental concern, and these images and campaigns from their childhoods are my informants' earliest memories of pro-environmental practices and of feeling like they could "do their part" for the environment.

In 2011, the city of Portland switched from weekly to every-other-week trash pickup with weekly recycling pickup, justifying this change by allowing residents to begin putting food scraps into the yard waste bins (Sarasohn 2011). While this took some getting used to for some households, the response among my informants was positive.

Amy: I think a good aspect of Portland is that there are a lot of monetary incentives for being more environmentally conscious, which I think will help motivate people who may not be leaning toward it just for the sake of doing it. But just making it easier with the trash situation, making it more expensive to have more trash pickup or bigger cans. In [Texas] you have this HUGE trash can that gets picked up every week, you get a tiny recycling box that picks up every other week, and there's no composting. We are finally living someplace that was more in line with what we wanted, which was the big recycling can and the small trash can.

Andrew: The thing that was so beautiful about it was how symmetric it is. You know, it was literally the exact opposite. In terms of which size different cans are and the frequency of pickup.

Brian: I'm kind of a passive supporter of the way that the city has pushed down trash in relation to recycling. So, making it less frequent pickup, making it smaller containers, trying to push more into the recycling stream … And I've got past the point where every other week trash collection was an issue, and if I forget on a particular week [to take out the trash] it's not a problem. So, my overall level of trash has just continued to decline

They like that the city is encouraging people to recycle and compost through these kinds of "incentives" and policies that make sending things to the landfill more expensive or difficult. This policy change reflected my informants' belief that the city makes decisions about how to get things done—at least some of the time—that are consistent with the values and priorities of my informants.

When I asked informants about trash in general, only Gloria expressed strong emotions.

Gloria: Throwing stuff away really affects me. I don't like throwing stuff away. It makes me feel ungracious and greedy and truly guilty. Spoiled! Because I know where it's going. It's never actually going away.

For most of my informants, some quantity of soiled, contaminated, or no longer useful items are a fact of life. However, informants in nearly every household I spoke with brought up the topic of "packaging" without being asked, and I was surprised by the intensity of their negative reaction to packaging. What they mean by packaging is the things—whether recyclable or not—that surround the products they buy to protect them for transportation and distribution. This includes materials like cardboard boxes that online purchases come in, plastic films, plastic bags, and rigid plastic clamshell containers. Avoiding packaging in items they buy is something that many of the households I spoke with put active effort into.

Brian: I do pretty actively make choices on purchases based on low levels of packaging, low levels of creating a lot of that waste.

Chris: I'm always buying bulk and trying to avoid buying stuff that's in clamshells or things like that. And then for other items, like if you're getting sandwich bread we will save the bags and reuse them for other stuff. We use a lot of yogurt containers and things like that for food storage later.

Scott: We've been doing Blue Apron [recipe and meal delivery service] for a few months, but I think we are going to stop that because of all the packaging. The food service is a real benefit because it helps us avoid wasting food. I think we're going to switch to Sun Basket, which is a similar service, but with purely recyclable and compostable packaging. The freezer packs are just water and cotton.

Eric: I think we got Blue Apron [recipe and meal delivery service] for a month or two. It was just way too much packaging. They tout that it is pre-portioned to avoid waste, and everything's recyclable, and it's not. Like, no. After like a month or two of that, I was disgusted with it. It is *so wasteful*. Our situation is not unique. A lot of people are in this situation in terms of how the limited time, and us trying to survive, and sustainability intersect. That's one of the ways it did. We make a decision in terms of sustainability when we decided to cancel Blue Apron.

Eric is a person whose wife describes him as "super laid-back and chill." He has a pleasant, friendly, and go-with-the-flow demeanor, but I could hear genuine anger and frustration in his voice every time he brought up packaging. He was able to eliminate this one source of packaging from his household when he cancelled a meal delivery service, but it is hard to avoid packaging when buying both food and other consumer goods, particularly as a parent.

Amy: It's hard to spend the extra time and money on making sure you consume less plastic. Everything is in a plastic thing, and then it's in a box, and then it's …

Carrie: Toys always have so much packaging and weird plastic parts, and it is harder to come buy stuff like that without a lot of packaging.

Tim: They are feeding kids this constant drip of snacks. Morning snack, afternoon snack, "Where's my snack?" I'm bummed that it's a bunch of gummies most of the time, and its wrapper is its own negative impact on the ecosystem. Oil, plastic lining, and a bunch of ink. It's just silly.

Several informants told me that one of the biggest changes in their habits since becoming a parent is purchasing large quantities of packaged snacks for their children. They feel bad about the packaging associated with feeding their children this way, but for many households, the alternative—making all snack food items for their children from scratch or portioning out foods from a larger container into smaller reusable containers—takes too much time.

My informant Fiona is a low-income single mother of two who does not own a car and lives in a small apartment without air conditioning. According to Fiona, out of all of her actions that could be harmful for the environment, she believes that the packaging surrounding the food she buys has the biggest adverse effect.

Fiona: I feel that our biggest negative environmental impact is food packaging, for sure.

Similarly, Rob told me point-blank that he does not like packaging, and Eric says that plastic packaging is the thing that bothers him the most.

Rob: I do not like packaging waste and things of that nature.

Eric: Plastic is probably the thing that gets under my skin more than
          anything else. Whenever I go to the grocery store, I never put
          any of the produce in plastic. I just put it in the cart and put
          it on the belt. I can tell some people are really put off by that.

Packaging is reviled. It is a necessary evil, a cost associated with provisioning
that protects purchases from damage and spoilage as they travel to their
final destination. Chris and Fiona try to reuse elements of packaging for
storage, but in general packaging serves no useful purpose once items arrive.
Packaging feels unnecessary and excessive, and it accumulates quickly in a
busy household. Packaging is a reminder to my informants of the futility of
many of their sustainability practices, a symbol of their lack of control, their
participation in consumer culture, and their collusion with the economic
institutions they oppose. The strong negative responses to packaging are
perhaps a displacement of a reality far too upsetting to acknowledge—that
the most sustainable option would be not existing at all.

Recycling

When I asked Yvonne, an urban homesteader who buys close to nothing
new and runs a permaculture business with her husband, about the
most important thing pro-environmental thing she does, her answer was
immediate: recycling. For many of my informants, recycling provokes
an emotional reaction opposite to the one elicited by packaging. People
love recycling. The inverse of negative images of litter and landfills and
strangulated birds from their childhoods, recycling was associated with
powerful memories and positive feelings of making a difference in the world.

Orla: The environment and environmental causes were big from a
          young age in school. The whole Reduce, Reuse, Recycle. It
          is now *painful* to me to not recycle something.

Both Penny and Quinn were involved in recycling volunteer projects during
high school in the early 1990s. Quinn went to a local recycling center to
help out on weekends, and Penny and some friends organized paper and
aluminum can recycling at their school, which had no recycling program
prior to their efforts. Some respondents' families of origin participated in
curbside recycling programs growing up, while others have memories of
their ecologically oriented parents driving their recyclable waste to the
closest processing center. Nicole remembers spending summers collecting
discarded beer cans off the beach and earning pocket money by returning
them. Some informants did not grow up recycling, and curbside recycling
has only recently become available in the places where they grew up.

Recycling is a universal practice in the households I spoke with. In fact, *not* recycling was considered socially taboo.

Rebecca: Here, everyone recycles. Not recycling is on the same
            level as spanking here. If someone told me here that they
            don't recycle, I'd be like, "What?!? That is antiquated and
            NOT ok!"
Tara: Everyone recycles in Portland. If someone told me that
            they don't recycle, it would be shocking. For me, I think
            what would be hard about that would be knowing the
            shame associated with not knowing any better. Maybe
            they haven't had anyone who taught them, and then they
            are feeling judged.

Owen compared the practice of recycling in Portland to churchgoing in his Midwestern hometown. It is just something you do to let everyone in your community know that you're a decent human being.

Owen: I don't want to throw a ton of stuff in a landfill or
            be wasteful, but there is also a social norm aspect
            to recycling.

When my informants talked about recycling, they were generally referring to two things—curbside recycling and bottle return. Curbside recycling involves sorting recyclable items into a separate bin for weekly home pickup by a waste disposal service, while bottle return involves taking certain items, like aluminum cans and glass bottles, to a machine at a grocery store for a return of the deposit paid at the time of purchase. Items with a bottle return deposit can be recycled at the curbside, but doing so forfeits the deposit. Only two of my informants talked to me about participating in bottle return. While Mina is in charge of curbside recycling and nearly all of her household's sustainability practices, bottle return is Mike's chore. He views it as a separate activity from recycling, and it is his job to collect aluminum cans and beer bottles and return them to the store for the deposits. Nathan and Nicole have a personal assistant who helps them with various chores for twenty hours a week, and returning cans and bottles is one of his jobs, though he does not get to keep the money from the deposits.

Everyone I spoke with participates in curbside recycling, though they have different levels of investment in recycling rules. Sorting recycling properly takes time and know-how. Many respondents admit that they find it difficult to keep track of which items are recyclable, and that they find the rules occasionally counterintuitive.

Quinn:	It seems like some of the things I'd like to put in the recycling, I've found out that they can't take in the curbside recycling. Plastic strawberry containers are an example of that. You have to take that to a special recycling place.
Kirstin:	How do you learn about what can be recycled and not?
Carrie:	[laughs]
Chris:	It's such a pain in the neck. I feel like it changes a lot. We get the thing [mailer] from Metro [regional government] annually, and ...
Carrie:	There are still certain plastic pieces that I'm never quite sure ...
Chris:	We used to just keep that thing around, but I feel like we've just ...
Carrie:	Oh, the guide?
Chris:	Yeah, the guide. But I feel like we've just gotten into a routine about what stuff is recyclable or not. But I know that they've increased some things.
Carrie:	Yeah, there's certain plastics that I throw out that probably ...
Chris:	You know, the plastic lids ... that can now go on top of the whatever plastic containers ...
Carrie:	[laughing] I could use more education on the specific plastic items.

Some of the more committed recyclers seek out information and educate themselves on proper recycling, which requires both investing time and knowing where to look to find this information in the first place. Dayna can get this information from her workplace, where she learns sustainability skills on the job that that are also helpful when she is at home.

Brian:	I learn about what is recyclable from Metro! I actually really pay attention to those things! I hear also the local and national media about how recycling works, and I've heard things like the fact that the quality of recycled paper is going down because of mixed stream recycling. So, it really is important for you to keep your food-related crap out of the recycling! So just kind of general news research, and then the local notifications and educational campaigns and that kind of thing. I actively seek out information, but I also actually read the information that's sent to me! [laughing]
Kirstin:	How do you find out about recycling sorting?
Dayna:	I tell David how it is, and he tries to disagree with the rules! [laughing] About what's recyclable and how to sort? I rely on people that I know who are like Master Recyclers and have taught me what is recyclable and we have some folks

in our office who have done a great job of educating, and there is always the guide from the city.

In many households, there is one member of a couple who is more invested in recycling and the rules of recycling than the other. Dayna and David's conflicts over recycling will be discussed in more detail in Chapter 8. Quinn says that she is more "anal" about recycling, and will take the extra effort to rip plastic pieces off cardboard packaging so the cardboard can be recycled. Nicole sorts through the recycling to correct what she believes to be recycling errors that Nathan has made, and Leonda picks recyclable items out of the trash that their roommate and husband have discarded.

Recyclable items that can't be recycled via the curbside system can still be recycled through non-curbside recycling. Some informants, like Ivy and Eric, take items to New Seasons, a local natural foods store that provides recycling processing of items that aren't accepted through curbside recycling. Penny takes items, including not just packaging but also broken plastic toys, to a local for-profit recycling center that accepts a larger number of items than can be recycled at the curbside. Several other households wish they could practice non-curbside recycling, but they don't feel that they have the time for this extra chore.

Chris: You can take certain things over to Far West Fibers [for-profit recycling center], but then the added effort is usually an impediment.

Rebecca: There is not really time during the weekend between grocery shopping and kids' activities to make a special trip to the recycling center, but down the line I can see that those are things that we would want to do. Right now, we are prioritizing sanity.

Amy: We don't typically take the plastic bags in. Like I know you can do it to grocery stores, but that extra step doesn't seem to happen very easily.

Many of my informants are passionate about recycling. They like the idea of their waste having another life after it is no longer useful to them, and it alleviates their guilt related to consumption.

Emily: I always feel a little guilty when I get something from Amazon or something that is egregiously packaged. We just do our best to recycle the components.

While Yvonne believes that recycling is the most important thing her household does for the environment, Kelly believes that recycling is the most insignificant pro-environmental practice a person can engage in.

Kelly: I think recycling is a rather small drop in the bucket of how we are affecting the environment. I saw a bumper sticker recently that said, "Recycling: It really is the least you can do." And I think, yes, that's true it really is the least we can do. And Portland makes it ridiculously easy.

For several informants, recycling waste is not sufficient for them to feel absolved.

Eric: I think we are pretty good on the post-processing end. But we could definitely take some steps on the pre-end. For example, I took all the film stuff to New Seasons [local natural food store] the other night. And as I was going through the process of recycling it, I am thinking to myself, "This is too much." Even though we're recycling it in this way. So that's something that's been on my mind as an opportunity as a household to improve.

Orla: We go through a lot of apple sauce pouches. We recycle them, but it would be nice to not buy them in the first place.

Penny: I will take plastic things to the special recycling place, including toys, just all plastic that isn't curbside recycled I take over there. But I did some research and found out that they just ship it to China. So, then it is going on a boat across the world, and maybe not great things are happening with it.

Fiona: If I'm buying something I try to think about if the packaging is something that I can reuse as opposed to just recycle because I know that even recycling takes energy.

These informants realize that there are environmental costs associated with producing and recycling these materials, and the best option would be neither recycling nor sending materials to the landfill. They would prefer to not generate this waste in the first place but are constrained in their ability to avoid all waste-generating consumption.

Composting

When my informants talked about compost, what they meant was food scraps and food-soiled paper that is diverted from landfills and allowed to decompose into soil. Only a few of my informants grew up composting, and those who did had parents who were particularly ecologically minded.

Tim: We composted growing up, but it meant that my first experience being attacked by animals was because I was walking around in my backyard and I stepped on a hornet's nest in this garbage pile.

Composting was sometimes a way to divert waste from landfills, and sometimes, as in Tim's case, as a way to produce fertilizer to enrich the soil so his parents could grow vegetables.

At the same time as trash pickup was changed to every other week, Portland began allowing residents to put food waste and food-soiled paper into their yard waste bin for weekly pickup (Sarasohn 2011). Informants living in single-family homes in Portland take advantage of curbside composting, though some of them also use backyard composting systems. Ian and David spoke specifically about putting bones and other things that are not good for backyard compost into the city curbside compost.

Ian: We do a little bit of the city compost for bones and bread, and then we have a backyard compost for the good stuff, all of our vegetables.

Renters and owners of attached homes, like Brian, Fiona, and Tim and Tara, did not have access to composting. Tim diverts this waste from the landfill by saving it to use for broth, which he also sees as an important learning opportunity for his son, who lives with them on weekends.

Tim: We keep all of our vegetable waste and bones to make broth out of. I want my kid to see us using the whole plant and animal to show him some alternatives what he gets at his mom's house—ripping off the plastic wrap and digging in.

Brian says that because he doesn't have access to curbside composting, he uses the garbage disposal in his townhome instead of throwing food in the trash.

Brian: Rather than it [food waste] going into the garbage, most of the food waste that can goes down my garbage disposal and weighs down the water treatment plants. [laughing] That's the trade-off. But it's kind of staying more in that biosphere, rather than going to the dump.

Mike and Mina live in the suburbs between 30 and 45 minutes outside Portland, and the area where they live doesn't offer curbside composting. They recently ordered a subsidized backyard composting system from Metro, the regional government. Mina is new to many sustainability practices, so the backyard vegetable garden she is planting will be her first, and she is looking forward to using the compost as fertilizer.

Dayna and David and Heather feed food scraps and waste to their backyard chickens rather than throwing this waste into the trash or curbside compost.

David: We've had a backyard composting thing since we moved into this house ten years ago, and then when the city composting came along, that was quite helpful because there were certain things that we couldn't put in our backyard compost like meat and bones, and we could get that and put it in the city compost. And then the chickens are our zero-waste system.

Dayna: And you don't have to feel guilty that we didn't get to the bottom of that sour cream container and it went off.

For Dayna and David, their three-pronged approach to composting alleviates some of the guilt associated with wasting food that has spoiled or they can't finish.

Diapers

An unavoidable part of being a parent of young children is dealing with the waste of an infant who isn't yet toilet trained. Victor and Vanessa were able to mostly avoid diapers altogether by practicing assisted infant toilet training or "elimination communication" (Gross-Loh 2009). Because Vanessa, a stay-at-home parent, practiced attachment parenting, she was able to toilet train her children at a few months old. When they did use diapers, they used a disposable eco-friendly brand. This is an incredibly time-intensive practice, as it involves closely monitoring the infant at all times for the subtle signs that it might need to eliminate, and then holding the baby over a sink or toilet so it can relieve itself. For the rest of the households, the choice was between eco-friendly disposable diapers, cloth diapers washed at home, and cloth diapers washed via a delivery diaper-washing service. To break the practice of diapering down even further, cloth diapers washed at home could be machine washed and machine-dried or machine washed and line-dried. Some households also installed additional equipment in their homes like spray hoses to help with pre-washing the diapers, and researched the best soaps for washing the diapers. This topic tended to come up mostly with parents whose children were still in diapers, while parents of older children focused on other topics.

For households with very young children the decision about whether or not to use cloth diapers was an important one. Households with a health priority and attachment-parenting philosophies are more concerned with the health impacts of disposable diapers on their babies or the idea that disposable diapers might not be comfortable. Households who are more concerned with the environment and avoiding waste tried to weigh the environmental impact of their diapering choices.

David and Dayna relied on a friend with similar values who had researched diapering. This friend was helpful in steering them toward the choice of cloth diapering and reduced some of the burden involved in learning about how to do cloth diapering. They also believe that cloth diapering is saving them money in the long run.

David: Our biggest thing that we've committed to reduce trash is the cloth diapers. It's an ongoing commitment.

Kirstin: Do you have a [diaper-washing] service?

Dayna: No, we do it ourselves, and it is definitely that you are sacrificing time and convenience.

David: Every couple days it's a pretty significant time investment to wash them and fold them.

The choice of cloth diapers, whether motivated by environmental or health concerns, requires a large investment of time. Cloth diapering also restricts which preschools and daycares a child can attend—this was an important factor for cloth-diapering families in selecting childcare providers. There is also an investment in materials required for cloth diapering. Using cloth diapers requires more than a set of at least 24 cloth diapers to get a newborn through two days between laundry loads, but also a diaper pail to hold soiled diapers, a wet bag to carry soiled diapers away from home, pins, inserts, and diaper covers (Wels 2011, 213). Fiona was able to obtain cloth diapers through a low-income diaper rental program, but made her own cloth diapers out of old clothes prior to that. Kelly installed a spray hose in her bathroom to help pre-wash diapers by rinsing off feces prior to laundering; this now doubles as an improvised bidet that allows her to go longer between showers.

Jim and Jess don't use their tumble dryer for environmental reasons, so they hang-dry cloth diapers year-round on racks that take up a substantial portion of their roughly 800 square foot home. David and Dayna hang-dry diapers in the summer, and believe that drying diapers in the sun gets them much cleaner than drying them in the tumble dryer. For Rob and Rebecca, having their cloth diapers cleaned through a commercial diaper service costs money but makes cloth diapering feasible for their household by helping them avoid some of the most time-intensive aspects of the practice.

Compared with cloth diapers, disposable diapers take much less time and don't require up-front investments in learning or materials. Heather wound up transitioning each of her children to eco-friendly disposable diapers to save time, though they all started out in cloth diapers. Fiona uses disposable diapers around 10 percent of the time for what she describes as an investment in her sanity, and Rob and Rebecca also use disposable diapers part of the time, particularly overnight. Fiona and Heather both told me that they feel bad about using disposable diapers on their children, and Rob and Rebecca disagreed on the proportion of disposable diapers that they use—Rebecca believes they use a higher proportion of cloth diapers than Rob does.

Jim and Jess spent a lot of time researching the impacts of cloth versus disposable diapers, and Jim now believes that he made the wrong decision, despite all of the research.

Jim: Cloth diapering was an environmental choice, and I think in retrospect that it was the wrong choice. Now I think disposable diapers are the better choice. But that's a good example of not being able to find good information and thinking we were making the right environmental choice. It was definitely a very conscious, researched choice. And I think I got it wrong. But we put a *lot* of thought into it.

The informants I spoke with who use cloth diapers are spending substantial amounts of time to do so because they are convinced that this is the best choice for their children and the environment. Though, as Jim points out, the facts are not clear and my informants are just doing the best they can to make the right decisions in spite of limited information, time, and money.

Toilet waste

"Selective flushing" is the practice of flushing the toilet following a bowel movement, but not flushing after urinating. While no one I spoke with had heard the term before, they all knew what I was talking about immediately and were familiar with the practice—people commonly call this practice, "If it's yellow, let it mellow. If it's brown, flush it down."

Quinn: I don't flush every time. If it's pee, we'll probably let it go three or four before we flush. If there's enough toilet paper in there and it's yellow and it starts to smell when it's hot outside, then it's time to flush.

Only a few of my informants grew up with selective flushing, and the ones who did frequently mentioned learning this practice during the 1987–1992 drought in California (California Department of Water Resources 1993). This experience of drought and the associated water-conservation practices spread to some of my informants who grew up in other regions via their contact with friends from California.

Scott: I remember being reprimanded by a buddy who was over watching me do dishes because I was just running the water, and he said, "You obviously didn't grow up in California when there was a drought."

Orla practiced selective flushing growing up in Oregon because her parents were driven to save money on their water bills, and Carrie grew up with selective flushing in a spiritual intentional community on the East Coast.

Carrie: Yeah, I learned about that growing up. And friends of mine that would like *never* flush and I'd be like, "Blarrrrrrg! Come on! We don't need to take it that far!"

For everyone else, selective flushing was something that they adopted as adults, often after being exposed to the practice through college roommates or other friends.

Fiona: That [selective flushing] was something that probably even in the past five years that I was exposed to, and I was like, "Oh, yeah! That makes sense." My sister lived with us for a while, and that's what *they* do. And that introduced me to that.

Kelly: We don't flush when we pee. I think I encountered that when I moved out here, and I thought, "OK that makes sense."

Tara: It's time to flush when you do a number two. We're not going to leave presents in there!

Leonda recalls first hearing about selective flushing from the 2004 comedy *Meet the Fockers*, which inspired them to adopt the practice to save water.

The practice was very common among my respondents, but not universal. Jim recalls encountering some resistance to his selective flushing practices when he moved to the East Coast after college.

Jim: I learned about [selective flushing] in college. I think it was a trendy thing to do. But when I moved to the East Coast, I attempted to selectively flush, and my roommates just thought it was disgusting. It was definitely not part of the culture over there.

Nicole knows some households who practice selective flushing, but she thinks not flushing the toilet for the environment is going too far.

Nicole: Selective flushing. Ew. I mean I get it, but ...

Dayna accepts but does not like selective flushing, and has a gender-based explanation.

Dayna: I am cool with "letting it mellow," but to a certain extent my threshold is just different from David's. For women, you are closer to the mellowing source so you are more aware of the smell than a guy generally is, because he has greater distance. So being in the miasma of the situation … yeah.

Tim also doesn't like selective flushing, and also has a gender-based explanation: he believes that men's urine smells worse than women's urine.

Tim: I flush every time because I feel like guy pee has some kind of marking our territory thing left over from our animal ancestors, so I think there is an odor that gets really crazy really fast.

Owen has trouble with selective flushing because he has memories of getting in trouble growing up for not flushing.

Owen: Orla is probably better at selective flushing than I am, because I grew up getting yelled at when I would forget to flush.

Eric and Emily and Ian and Ivy say that their children frequently forget to flush bowel movements, and that they need to remind them *to flush* rather than train them not to flush every time.

My informants have other water and resource-saving toilet practices beyond selective flushing. Because of their differences in tolerance for selective flushing, Dayna and David say they "solved that problem" by buying a dual-flush toilet that uses a small amount of water for liquid waste and larger amount of water for solid waste. Penny cut up old bed sheets to make washable toilet wipes for her daughter, a practice Mina refers to as "family cloth":

Mina: We don't do "family cloth" homemade toilet paper. That's a level we can't do.

Kyle and Kelly practice selective flushing, but they also put bottles inside the toilet tank to displace water, resulting in less water used in each flush. Kyle says they need to put some smaller bottles in the tanks, because he is finding himself having to flush twice sometimes to wash all of the solid waste out of the toilet bowl.

Selective flushing is an interesting sustainability practice because it doesn't involve buying anything and it doesn't involve additional effort—in fact it involves *not* doing something that is a common activity. Practicing selective flushing means relearning a hygiene habit taught to children as soon as they begin toilet training. The practice is not on display outside the home. Several two-adult households practicing selective flushing had never even discussed the habit among themselves—it had become an automatic and taken-for-granted practice for these informants by the time they arrived at the stage of forming a household with their partners. Ivy recently used a composting toilet on a friend's property and commented that the conventional way of dealing with human waste is actually quite strange.

Ivy: It weirds me out that we shit in clean water. We just went to a friend's farm, and they have a composting toilet. This is so much better than shitting in fresh water! Dumping water like that, it just doesn't make any sense.

Once people start looking into alternative ways of getting things done, the absurdities of taken-for-granted conventions and conventional practices become evident.

References
Aleiss, Angela (1999) "Iron Eyes Cody: Wannabe Indian," *Cinéaste*, 25(1): 31.
California Department of Water Resources (1993) "California's 1987–92 Drought: A Summary of Six Years of Drought," Available: https://web.archive.org/web/20170630135401/https://water.ca.gov/waterconditions/docs/2_drought-1987-92.pdf, 2017].
Cialdini, Robert B. (2001) "Littering: When every litter bit hurts," in Ronald E. Rice and Charles K. Atkin (eds) *Public Communication Campaigns*, Thousand Oaks, CA: SAGE.
Gross-Loh, Christine (2009) *The Diaper-Free Baby: The Natural Toilet Training Alternative*, New York: HarperCollins.
Kelly, Daniel (2011) *Yuck! The Nature and Moral Significance of Disgust*, Cambridge, MA: MIT Press.
Sarasohn, David (2011) "Biweekly Trash Pickup: Get to Know your Garbage," *The Oregonian*, December 10, Available: http://www.oregonlive.com/news/oregonian/david_sarasohn/index.ssf/2011/12/biweekly_trash_pickup_get_to_k.html [Accessed May 30, 2017].
Shabecoff, Philip (1987) "With No Room at the Dump, U.S. Faces a Garbage Crisis," *New York Times*, June 29, Available: http://www.nytimes.com/1987/06/29/us/with-no-room-at-the-dump-us-faces-a-garbage-crisis.html [Accessed May 30, 2017].
Weinbaum, Batya and Amy Bridges (1976) "The other side of the paycheck: Monopoly capital and the structure of capitalism," *Monthly Review*, 28(3): 88–103
Wels, Kelly (2011) *Changing Diapers: The Hip Mom's Guide to Modern Cloth Diapering*, South Paris, MA: Green Team Enterprises.

6

Cleanliness and Comfort

The social and cultural meanings of cleanliness and comfort have evolved over time, generally in ways that demand more resources (Shove 2003). The temperatures that feel comfortable indoors, and the actions people take and the equipment they use to remain comfortable, are matters of cultural expectations and social norms, but the equipment and infrastructures in homes recursively reinforces expectations about how people should feel indoors and what steps they ought to take to feel that way. And ironically, as new supposedly time-saving domestic technologies emerge, cleaning practices and the demand for cleanliness have changed in ways that demand more unwaged time rather than less (Cowan 1983). Changes in infrastructures and technologies, like central heating and in-home washing machines, make these evolutions in cultural expectations possible, and even recursively reinforce the normalcy of these expectations. So while cleanliness and comfort involve mundane habits that are easily taken for granted, my informants have made changes to conventional ways of getting things done to make their practices more sustainable. In some cases, these changes take more unwaged time (as Cowan 1983 documents) but in other cases these changes—intriguingly—result in less unwaged time devoted to mundane household practices.

Cleanliness

Shove (2003, 10) says that demand escalators don't run backwards, but the ways that my informants have changed their showering, laundry, and household cleaning habits provide concrete examples of very real demand-decreasing changes in practices *and* accompanying changes in the meaning of cleanliness. Some of these changes involve taking additional unwaged time to perform cleaning activities in more labor-intensive ways that avoid the use of energy or "chemicals," or purchasing special cleaning products, but other changes involve simply reducing the frequency of cleaning, thus actually reducing the amount of unwaged work involved.

Showering

The history of personal hygiene in the United States by Bushman and Bushman (1988) reveals that the meaning and practices associated with personal cleanliness have changed substantially since the 18th century, when even affluent Americans might never bathe, cleaning themselves instead with an occasional sponge bath—a wet cloth and no soap. The accompanying infrastructure—a washbasin—was still a fairly rare item to find in U.S. homes, and bathtubs were completely absent. By 1900, bathing practices had changed such that most Americans bathed fairly regularly, though still far less than we do today, as bodily cleanliness began to take on new social and moral meanings. In fact, the first soap for washing the body was only introduced around this time. Bushman and Bushman (1988, 1238) write that, "Now the wish to be clean feels more like a natural instinct than a cultural overlay." In questioning so many other taken-for-granted assumptions about how to get things done in everyday life, many of my informants have also changed the way they keep their bodies clean. Like selective flushing, practices that decrease the frequency of bathing are an intriguing sustainability practice. While short showers and low-flow showerheads allow a daily shower to become more efficient, showering less often is a way that my informants save resources, time, *and* money. The main cost is a social and cultural one, as bathing and cleanliness are saturated with deep cultural meanings.

The majority of my informants shower less frequently than they did growing up, and often this change was a deliberate one related to sustainability.

Quinn: I grew up with a daily shower, and now I take a quick shower every three or four days. It's probably about five years that I've been doing that.

Leonda: My husband and I shower probably once every week, and our roommate showers maybe once every two weeks. I remember one of the first times I was spending time around the environmental activists in my community, and I saw a woman across the room and she put her arms above her head, and there was hair there! I thought, "Wait, what? You can be a woman and not shave? That's so crazy!" So, I never shaved again after that.

Kyle: I shower every two or three days depending on the temperature and the smell-test. I used to be a daily showerer.

Kelly: Probably every three or four days. I'll do the pit wash. PTA in the sink [pits, tits, and ass]. We installed a spray hose for cloth diapers, and now it's sort of a bidet for me. I've considered getting a bidet attachment for the upstairs toilet. I feel like that's one reason to shower regularly. If you can actually clean your ass, you don't need to shower that much.

Exposure to nondominant cultural norms changed Leonda's perception of taken-for-granted personal grooming practices—once they realized there were alternatives, they changed their habits immediately. Kyle and Kelly use a spray hose they installed for cleaning cloth diapers as a bidet to allow them to go longer between showers and will do what they call a "PTA" sponge bath using a facecloth and the sink. Andrew and Amy are daily bike commuters, but take showers every two to three days.

Andrew: Yeah, with me I just go by how thick my stubble is. That's my measure for when I need to take a shower. Like oh yeah this is pretty thick. I need to go take a shower. Because that's when I shave.

Andrew decides when to shower based on a factor that has nothing to do with smell or a feeling of cleanliness—when his facial hair gets long enough that he wants to shave it.

A striking example of a demand escalator running backwards is the story of Tara's conversion from someone who would habitually take several showers a day to someone who now takes only one shower a day for environmental reasons.

Tara: When I was younger, I used to have no problem just showering three times a day. Wake up, shower. Go to the gym, shower. Going out that night, shower to get ready. It was no big deal to shower all the time! Now, I try my best to take fewer showers. I do take really short showers, but now I don't want to take a shower when I wake up just to take a shower again a few hours later after I exercise. Now, showering more than once a day seems excessive to me. But I used to take two or three showers every day. I grew up in this very excessive environment where you just do what you want when you want to do it. Now, being in Portland, I try to think about those things a little bit more. I don't feel comfortable without a daily shower, but I am trying to be mindful now so I'm not an excessive water user.

She still feels uncomfortable unless she has at least one shower, and she works in close proximity to her clients in the beauty industry, whom she doesn't want to offend with body odor. However, she has dramatically reduced her demand for hot water, and her views on when to shower and what being clean feels like have changed after moving to a place with different norms than where she grew up.

Some social norms around cleanliness are enforced by spouses. Ian has decreased the amount he showers compared to the daily shower he took as a teenager, but his wife would prefer him to bathe more frequently.

Ian: I was a daily showerer when I was a teenager, but I'm not anymore. Now maybe once every two days. Sometimes I push it …

Ivy: And then I get mad! I'm like "TAKE A SHOWER!" You smell.

While Ivy was laughing and joking around during the interview, it was clear that she does occasionally demand that Ian shower because she doesn't like his smell. Ivy showers daily, but she also mostly bikes to her office job a few miles away. For some of my informants, the sustainability practice of bike commuting causes an increase in demand for resources in another area by causing them to shower more frequently. Eric, Kyle, Brian, David, and Dayna all told me about showering at their workplaces following their bike commutes, a practice made possible by cycling-friendly employers who installed showers.

Other informants shower everyday so that they can smell and feel clean.

Tim: I will talk to people who tell me they only need a shower once every two weeks, but I do a bit of an internal eye-roll. Oh man, you DO need a shower, what do you mean? Good on you for not showering, but that is bad for me!

Heather: My husband is a more than once a day showerer. He showers once in the morning and once when he gets home. He has to be clean.

While there were still daily showerers—and some more than once daily showerers—among my informants, the overall bathing patterns here demonstrate that it is indeed possible to change the meaning of personal cleanliness and the methods that produce personal cleanliness in ways that decrease the consumption of resources like water and water heating.

Laundry

Like bathing, laundry has a cultural and technological history in the United States, and the mundane and habitual nature of laundry makes these changes easy to overlook. Shove (2003, 2004, 77) has pointed repeatedly to transitions in laundry practices as a valuable topic for research into "normality" and the implications that social and cultural norms have for the environment through the demands they place on resources like water and energy. The history of this evolution in U.S. laundry practices over time is instructive. Hoy (1996, 153) describes the prevalent laundry norms among the U.S. poor in the 1930s, when undergarments might be changed once a season, and other clothes washed weekly or even monthly. Working people had very few clothes at this time, and washing them was laborious, unpleasant, and time-consuming. Laundry is a recursive practice—the ease of washing and drying clothing makes having more clothes more appealing, and having more clothes you'd like to keep clean makes having a way to wash them more appealing. Parr (1997, 183) points out that the early users of automatic home washing machines took notice of the amount of resources these machines consumed, accustomed as they were to hauling and pumping water and monitoring their septic systems. Parr reports that in 1955, one Canadian housewife wrote:

> I have been appalled at the amount of water that seems necessary to do a normal family wash in the new spin-dry type of machine. I believe one brand boasted that it rinsed clothes seven times, and all of them threw the water out after one use. There is hardly a city or town in Canada that does not have some water shortage in summer months. Large sums are being spent on reforestation, conservation and dams. It would appear that this trend towards excessive use of water should be checked now.

Not every culture immediately accepts new laundry technologies and their associated practices—despite geographic and linguistic proximity, Canadians took decades longer to adopt automatic home washing machines than their U.S. counterparts (Parr 1997, 159).

There is more than one way to get clothes washing done, of course, and the history of laundry tells a story of a chore being transferred from the home to the commercial sector and then back into the home again (Watson 2015). Cowan (1983, 105–108) discusses commercial laundries, which used to be commonplace and used for at least part of the washing by most households as the demand for clean clothes increased in the late 19th and early 20th centuries, and this unpleasant and grueling domestic task was outsourced. Along with their reluctance to adopt automatic washing machines, Canadian households from all classes also made use of commercial clothes washing services well into the mid-20th century (Parr 1997, 173). Lynd and Lynd (1929) found that by the mid-1920s in Muncie, Indiana, the appearance of washing machines and electric irons in homes began to shift these laundry tasks from commercial laundries back into individual homes. This increase in home washing machines represents a socio-technological pattern that:

tends to perpetuate a questionable institutional set-up—whereby many individual homes repeat common tasks day after day in isolated units—by forcing back into the individual home a process that was following belatedly the trend in industry toward centralized operation. (Lynd & Lynd 1929, 175)

Cowan (1983, 110) points out that outsourced domestic washing is now generally reserved just for the dry cleaning of men's suits and button-up dress shirts. An exception to this tendency in my sample of households was Rob and Rebecca, who make use of a cloth diaper-washing service.

Shove (2003, 117) points out that, unlike showering, there are deep gender divisions in laundry practices. U.S. women spend over three times as much time doing laundry than men (U.S. Bureau of Labor Statistics 2016). There was some minor evidence in my discussions with informants that women in the heterosexual dual-earner households did more of the laundry than their husbands, though laundry did frequently appear to be an equally shared task. David apparently did not know what type of laundry detergent his household uses, and Dayna claimed that he had *never* purchased laundry detergent for their household. Heather told me that she does the laundry for their household, but she saw this chore as part of an egalitarian division of household tasks that involved specialization. She saw the assignment of the laundry chore to herself as an even trade, since her husband was in charge of doing the dishes and keeping the kitchen clean, a chore that Heather hates.

One way my informants integrated their sustainability priorities with their laundry practices was wearing clothing more than once between washings.

Fiona: I do laundry less often. I'll wear clothes again instead of just tossing them in the hamper.

Eric and Emily have been teaching their children to wear some clothes more than once at the same time as they are beginning to ask them to throw their dirty clothes down the laundry chute as a daily chore.

Eric: We try to communicate to the kids that they don't need to put their pajamas that they wore like from after they took a shower until when they woke up in the morning in the laundry. The idea that you can wear things a couple of times.
Emily: But that they *should* put their underwear in the laundry! [laughing]

While Eric and Emily's children struggle at times to understand the nuances of these distinctions, they are mature for their ages and keen to be helpful around the house. Amy's children are roughly the same age as Emily's, but she describes a different experience teaching her children their sustainability practices related to laundry.

Amy: Well, I do try to motivate the kids to not put their stuff in the laundry like every time they wear it, and that's kind of an ongoing battle, because they just want to kind of just chuck it into a basket and call it a day.

Amy interprets her children's tendency to put clothes into the laundry hamper after a single wear as laziness rather than a misdirected desire to be helpful and tidy. During our Saturday morning interview, Andrew and Amy's children were serious and quietly working on extracurricular foreign language exercises and math worksheets.

The choice of laundry soap between ecological and conventional alternatives was a topic that came up frequently in my conversations with informants. Emily uses a scent-free conventional soap because the natural soap she prefers was causing her high-efficiency washing machine to grow mold. Even though she is using a free-and-clear version of Tide [conventional] detergent, she told me that she was upset about having to switch to a conventional laundry soap. Orla and Owen have been using a scent-free ecological detergent since they moved into their current home. This is in part because of the sensitive skin of household members, and in part because the house isn't on the municipal sewer system and drains to a cesspool in the backyard. Using this soap has changed the associations Owen has with the scent of Tide detergent. Now, when he smells someone who washes their clothes with conventional detergents, he finds the scent very unpleasant. David and Dayna use Tide because they believe it is the most effective on cloth diapers following online research, while other households use Charlie's Soap [natural detergent] on their cloth diapers after researching the best soaps for washing diapers. Heather and Yvonne make their own laundry soap by adding Borax [sodium borate decahydrate] to bars of soap that they grate with a cheese grater. Yvonne isn't sure whether or not this is better for the environment, but she believes the large expenditure of time involved in grating bars of soap into flakes saves her household money. Penny used to make her own laundry soap in this way, but she decided she didn't believe it was more sustainable than commercially available natural laundry soaps. Leonda wishes they could make their own laundry soap, and has friends who do this, but feels like they don't have enough time.

Clothes dryers are ubiquitous in the United States—79 percent of all U.S. households own and use a tumble dryer at home, compared with 57 percent in the United Kingdom (U.K. Office for National Statistics 2011) and 4 percent in Italy (Project Laundry List 2013). And 97 percent of U.S. households in detached single-family homes own and use a tumble dryer

(U.S. Energy Information Administration 2013). But the mere existence of the tumble dryer in a home doesn't tell the whole story. While over half of U.K. households own a tumble dryer, 93 percent line-dry their laundry, while only 6–12 percent of U.S. households air-dry their clothes (Project Laundry List 2013). Shove (2003, 152–153) writes about the social meanings of line-dried laundry for the majority of U.K. households that strongly prefer it—hanging up the wash is enjoyable, the laundry smells better, and it is fresher and cleaner. An English interview subject reports feeling guilty for using the tumble dryer (Shove 2003, 152). These same associations and meanings with line-dried laundry are not prevalent in the U.S. context, though some of my informants, almost always contrary to the way they were raised, have started to line-dry their laundry for environmental reasons.

Jim and Jess line-dry all of their laundry, including sheets and towels, year-round. They have two large drying racks that they use for clothes, and they dry their bedlinens by hanging them over doorframes. They made the deliberate choice to live in an 800 square foot home, and the drying racks take up a lot of space inside.

Jim: Line drying is a conscious environmental decision because the dryer is a huge user of energy. It's probably one of the bigger things that we do. It's a big time commitment. We use two big drying racks in our room, and sheets and towels go over the doors around the house. It's a compromise because this is such a small house it takes up quite a bit of space in our room.

Line drying clothing year-round takes more time than drying clothes using a tumble dryer, but the environmental impact of this choice makes the trade-off worthwhile for Jim and Jess. Because the Portland area is so frequently rainy, Penny, David, and Dayna line-dry their clothes only during the relatively dry summers. When I asked the technologically oriented Dayna, a scientist by training, how she learned about line-drying laundry and what know-how and equipment were involved, she looked at me quizzically.

Kirstin: Did you research line-drying before you did it?
Dayna: Is there research to research?
Kirstin: Well, there's equipment involved, right?
Dayna: Ours is a retractable string from Fred Meyer [grocery store chain]. It was like five dollars.

This was an interviewing blunder I made early in the interviewing process—for Dayna, unlike for a social researcher, equipment means complex technologies, not a five-dollar string. Neither Dayna nor David grew up line-drying their laundry, and in fact they believed their parents would be hostile to the idea of line-drying. Dayna recalled her grandmother line-drying clothes when she'd visit her in Florida growing up and called her a "big believer" in drying clothes this way. Still, this was a lost practice that Dayna had to relearn, readopt, and restore for her own household. Rilke (1968 [1908], 334) writes in a letter to his wife about

> the first state of bliss: when a much earlier thing is given back to one so that one may grasp it and take it to oneself with a love meantime become more just. Here begins the revision of categories, where something past comes again, as though out of the future; something formerly accomplished as something to be completed.

Many of my informants' sustainability practices are practices that have sat dormant for a generation or two, only to reemerge with new significance and cultural meanings.

Andrew, Chris, Carrie, and Rob told me that they line-dry only certain things sometimes—this is just for delicate items or items informants really want to last.

Andrew: The reason I dry some of my clothes outside of the dryer is mainly because I don't want them to shrink. It's not really as much sustainability motivated as much just about the clothes.

In the suburb where Nathan and Nicole live, there are regulations against line-drying clothes. They line-dry items associated with Nicole's five dogs, mostly beds and towels, but they must do so in an area that is not visible from the road. Nathan grew up line-drying everything year-round, but now he prefers to put his clothes, towels, and bedlinens in the tumble dryer. He is worried that line-drying these items will cause them to attract pollen that will trigger his allergies.

While sustainability practices that involve washing clothes less often mean that households can spend less time doing laundry, line-drying clothing winds up taking more time and effort than drying clothes quickly in a tumble dryer. The time required to line-dry laundry is a major barrier for some households, even Heather's, with two adults who were accustomed to having line-dried clothes when they lived in England.

Heather: In California, I'd have some drying racks outside, but it was always sunny. But here, we've only been in Portland for a couple years. But to be honest, hang-drying clothes takes a lot of work and a lot more time. And now that there's five of us, there is a *lot* more laundry.

But beyond time spent or saved to conserve resources, there are other consequences to making sustainability-oriented changes to laundry practices. Changing laundry soap, washing clothes less, and line-drying clothes all involve changes to expectations and the cultural meaning of cleanliness for my informants as they strive to make choices that are healthier for their families and the environment.

Household cleaning

Three households told me that they had housekeeping help—Rob and Rebecca, Scott and Sarah, and Nathan and Nicole—substituting a purchased input for their own unwaged time. Not coincidentally, these were among the highest-income households in my sample. Other households may have had this help, but they did not volunteer this information. From the way my informants talked about cleaning, I did not get the impression that many had paid cleaning services. Kyle and Kelly live in intentional community, so all household chores are rotated through the five adults living in the home. Leonda and their husband live with a roommate, but the roommate doesn't contribute much by way of helping with household chores. While Victor and Vanessa live in a cohousing community, an aspect that Victor likes about this living arrangement is the fact that the chores on the outside of the home like yardwork are shared by his community, but the chores on the inside of the home are done by his wife. While there are different ways of arranging the work of household cleaning, most of my informants arranged this work in a conventional way—by doing it themselves.

As with laundry, there are gender divisions in the assignment of tasks related to household cleaning in the United States that were apparent in some of my conversations with informants.

Dayna: We have a mix of what I would consider earth-friendly stuff and then some not-so-earth-friendly stuff.
Kirstin: Where does the not-earth-friendly stuff go?
Dayna: When I think it is required.
David: What would that even be, like bleach?

David's seeming ignorance of both the type of laundry detergent, discussed earlier, and the household cleaning products and methods betrays his likely lack of involvement in this area of household work. However, this did not appear to be the norm for the households I spoke with who had two working adults in a heterosexual relationship.

The primary connection between sustainability practices and household cleaning my informants made involved the selection of products and methods for cleaning. A common theme among my informants was a belief that conventional cleaning products are able to clean more effectively and faster than more ecologically friendly alternatives, which they believe either don't work or require more effort. Dayna doesn't believe that nontoxic Bon Ami brand abrasive scrub can be a "natural" alternative to bleach-based scouring products because it is so effective, and initially listed it among the conventional products her household uses for cleaning.

Mina: I fully believe that vinegar, baking soda, and hydrogen peroxide can take care of anything. In the dishwasher is my only concession for using a conventional product. Seventh Generation was too much of a compromise and it was not getting things clean. It wasn't working.

Amy: I still use something for the toilet that's not just necessarily just vinegar and baking soda. I guess for me the toilet is just like a grosser place and I want to make sure I'm getting the bacteria and E. coli aspect of it, but also probably effectiveness and ability to do it quickly as well.

When more natural products fail or the job triggers fears of contamination, harsher conventional products are needed. These conventional products are believed to save time and effort.

Several households claimed to use exclusively natural cleaning products, and then when asked specifically about bathrooms admitted to using conventional products on toilets and in the bathroom.

Chris: For cleaning the house I have a grapefruit cleansing thing-a-ma-bobber.

Carrie: And like if we wash … the few times a year we actually mop our floors, mostly we might just use vinegar or water.

Chris: Maybe a little dish soap or something.

Carrie: Nothing too …

Chris: Mostly we just vacuum.

Kirstin: What about in the bathroom?

Carrie: We have a few kind of mildew stain type things we use in the bathroom.

Chris: Yeah, we'll bleach the shower.

Kirstin: So you use more conventional products in the bathroom?

Carrie: Yeaaaah.

This pattern of additional interview probing after an informant claimed to use exclusively natural products took place in several interviews.

Heather: Cleaning products would be something that I choose and that we make. I make my own laundry detergent, and we try to do that mindfully by using the Environmental Working Group website. I make my own shower sprays, I make my own counter cleaners. We make our own bug sprays. Out of essential oils, white vinegar, baking soda.

Kirstin: What about the toilet?

Heather: For the inside of the toilet, I use a conventional bleach-based gel but the outside of the toilet I use my own products that I make. For the dishwasher, I use a Seventh Generation pod. We buy dish soap that he picks up at Trader Joe's [moderately priced alternative grocery store chain with a cult following]. For the floors we use almond oil. We don't use anything else.

For most of my informants who prefer to use natural cleaning products, toilets and bathrooms are areas that require conventional products with disinfecting properties. Ian and Ivy were an exception. They tend not to use cleaning products at all, whether in the toilet or anywhere else in the house. She says that elbow grease is enough to get the job done.

Ivy: We honestly rarely use soap on the toilet. If we do, it is like Seventh Generation. But I just scrub it once a week, and I feel like that gets it pretty clean. Eight years ago, I bought a bottle of bleach and we've had that same bottle. And I will use that on mold. And I feel like I've used it maybe three times.

While the toilet and bathrooms aren't the triggers for disinfecting products, the appearance of mold does drive Ian and Ivy to use bleach.

Jim doesn't mind using conventional cleaning products for everything because he believes they make the job quicker and he is mostly concerned with the "footprint" of his choices on the natural environment and public health.

Jim: I do not make environmental decisions for household cleaning products. I definitely prefer cleaning with bleach and cleaning with nasty chemicals. My feeling is that it is such a small footprint, so it is OK. It is just more effective and a way to get the house cleaner.

Jim's value system and sustainability priorities mean that the environmental benefits of ecologically friendly household cleaning products—which he sees as less effective—are not worth the trade-offs involved.

In household cleaning, as in other facets of everyday life, my informants make trade-offs between priorities to get things done using the resources available to them and subject to the factors that constrain them. Households with strong sustainability priorities in the personal health arena take the extra time to use, and sometimes even produce, natural cleaning products in their homes. However, many households find that their cultural expectations for cleanliness take precedence over their health-related sustainability concerns and influence their decision to use conventional disinfecting products in the bathroom. Other households, particularly ones who are most concerned with the carbon impacts of their choices or not wasting resources, decide to save time by using conventional cleaning products. Other households use even more time and effort to clean with no products at all, or use their wages to purchase cleaning services so their time can be used elsewhere. The possible combinations of priorities, resources, and constraints used to produce cleanliness in sustainable households are seemingly boundless.

Comfort

Much like cleanliness, the production and social meanings of indoor comfort have changed over time and are not consistent across cultures. By comfort what I mean is the practices, materials, meanings, and infrastructures involved in feeling like you are at a comfortable temperature when you are inside, a notion borrowed from Shove (2003). During cold months, being comfortable might involve some combination of adjusting a thermostat connected to central heating, using portable space heaters, putting on additional clothing, drinking warm drinks or alcohol, sitting under blankets, putting on a fire, or congregating in a single room. During warm months, being comfortable might involve some combination of adjusting a thermostat connected to central air conditioning, using window or portable air-conditioning units, using electric fans or swamp coolers, opening and closing windows and blinds, wearing fewer clothes, cutting your hair short or wearing your hair up, taking a cold shower, drinking cold drinks, going to the river or public splash pads or pool, running through the sprinklers, taking a nap, or going to the movies or an air-conditioned shopping center.

Comfort when it's cold outside
Temperatures

Common indoor temperatures during cold weather were between 68 and 70 degrees Fahrenheit (20 and 21.1 degrees Celsius) on the high end and between 64 and 66 degrees Fahrenheit (17.8 and 18.9 degrees Celsius) on the low end for awake-and-home temperatures, though some of the extremes were 74 degrees Fahrenheit (23.3 degrees Celsius) on the high end and Ian and Ivy's unheated home, which Ivy thinks gets into the 50s Fahrenheit (10 to 15 degrees Celsius) and below, on the low end. Some households turn their heat all the way off at night and when they are not home because their home is so well insulated, and some households use no evening or away thermostat "set back" temperature at all. Other households set the temperature back a few degrees, and Orla and David and Dayna researched the optimal setbacks for their particular heating systems and homes.

There was a 10-degree Fahrenheit range—from 64 to 74 degrees Fahrenheit (17.8 to 23.3 degrees Celsius)—between the temperatures at which my informants told me they feel most comfortable in the winter. Sometimes these optimal comfort temperatures were different between members of a couple.

Heather: Because my husband is from England, he prefers it to be cold. If it's hot out, he is complaining. Even 70 degrees [Fahrenheit, or 21.1 degrees Celsius] he starts to complain. We are OK with 70 inside during the winter, but at that temperature, the front door is open, windows stay open, the basement door is open. I feel a draft! When it is cold outside, it does not affect him to even think about closing doors and windows.

These differences generally meant that the member of the couple who would prefer it to be warmer inside needed to take adaptive steps to remain comfortable, though not always. Heather's husband leaves doors and windows open during the winter to keep it a bit cooler than the thermostat setting that Heather prefers. Fiona tells me she likes it very warm during the winter, and she and her child were wearing short-sleeved shirts and shorts inside on a cool spring day.

Fiona: I feel like my tendency toward comfort is stronger than other people than I know. Like everyone in my family keeps their house colder than I do. You can see that the baby and I are both in T-shirts right now, and I still feel flushed and hot. I think that I like my house warmer, and I don't feel as comfortable bundled up in my house.

My informants ascribed these differences in comfort temperatures to some combination of biology, habits related to how and where they grew up, and personal preference.

Equipment

Most, but not all, of my informants had electric or natural gas central heating in their homes—a furnace or a heat pump. Nathan installed a costly geothermal system, in part because he calculated that it was cost-effective, and in part because he likes the technology.

Nathan: We have geothermal heating and cooling. It is a really high-
            efficiency rating system. Both radiant floor and forced air.
            It is totally cool.

His entire demeanor changed when he was talking about the system. Describing his geothermal system to me, Nathan sounded like an excited child describing a toy rather than an adult describing a home heating and cooling system costing tens of thousands of dollars. Nathan enjoys technology for its own sake, but also for the environmental potential of this technology.

Renters Leonda, Tim and Tara, and Fiona have electric baseboard heat, so they never really know what temperature it is inside, though Leonda and Fiona tell me that they keep it quite warm, and Tim and Tara try to heat their apartment as little as possible. Ian and Ivy's home has no central heating, and baseboard heating in only one room—their daughter's.

Ivy: We don't have a heating system in the house. In the winter
            overnight, it's probably in the 50s [Fahrenheit, or 10 to
            15 degrees Celsius]. It's really cold. I put on blankets and
            don't move from that spot on the sofa and read there. Our
            bedroom is in the attic, so it is very subject to the elements.
            I've always been pretty whiny about it. I make a big fuss
            about it, but I don't really do anything about it either.

The result is that Ivy is very uncomfortable in the evenings during the winter, and huddles under a duvet in the living room from when she gets home from work until it is time to go to sleep. She describes herself as "whiny" for wishing the home had functioning heat. Scott uses a space heater under his desk in his office when he's working from home, and Jim and Jess use a space heater to keep the overnight temperature in their child's room warmer than the temperature that they'd prefer for themselves. Kyle likes to use a space heater in a small space to make the temperature "luxurious" sometimes.

Investments in insulation, weather-stripping, and double-paned windows were fairly common, and these investments were seen as helping keep the temperature comfortable inside during both hot and cold weather. One of the first things that Andrew and Amy did when they moved into their home was replace the original windows with more efficient ones that could open and close, as the original windows had been painted shut. Kyle also replaced windows early on in his home renovations, and Mike and Mina say that the next project in their new home will be window replacement. Orla, however, decided that replacing windows wouldn't be cost-effective and instead focused on adding extra insulation to the walls and attic. All of the households who made energy-efficiency improvements took advantage of available tax incentives and other rebates, though generally my informants had already decided to make the improvements regardless of the incentives.

Actions

One way that my informants stay comfortable when it is cold out is to use their heating systems and space heaters. Most of the households I spoke with have programmed thermostats that run on a set schedule, and sometimes my informants adjust the settings when the regular program is making them feel too hot or too cold. Tim and Tara say they run their heat just to take the bite out of the air, and set their baseboard heaters "to the first click." They try to occupy the same room in their apartment when they are home, to avoid heating more than one space at a time.

Fires and gas fireplace inserts were also a popular way to heat homes, used fairly regularly by Andrew and Amy and Jim and Jess.

Jim: We try to heat with the fireplace as much as possible.
Jess: And I'm conflicted because it generates a lot of particulate matter.
Jim: We don't really know if it's the right choice or not, but I feel
         that from a climate perspective it is a better choice. But from a
         particulate matter perspective, it is not a better choice. But from
         a climate perspective, it is a better choice than our gas furnace.

Both of the households who use fires to heat their homes are conflicted about whether or not this is a good environmental choice. Quinn and Chris and Carrie and Scott and Sarah have natural gas fireplace inserts. Quinn enjoys sitting in front of the fireplace, though she says she knows it's "bad." Chris doesn't like it when his children put on the fire on cold mornings, because he believes it's wasteful and bad for the environment. Scott and Sarah mostly just use theirs when they have company over rather than just for their household members.

Some of my informants who live in homes with central heating would prefer to heat as little as possible or not at all, for some combination of environmental and financial reasons.

Gloria: I would prefer to not use the heat at all. I would prefer to put
          on my wool socks, and some sweatshirts.

Wendy didn't run the heat in her home at all until a colleague told her it was not good for her home and might cause mildew to grow on the house because of Oregon's damp climate. Quinn's husband also argues with her

111

about the thermostat settings, because Quinn would prefer it to be cooler in the home to save money and for environmental reasons. Her husband is an engineer, so they compromised because of his concerns about the integrity of the home at Quinn's preferred temperature.

My informants have ways of staying comfortable inside when it's cold out other than adjusting the thermostat or using auxiliary heaters. They talked about wearing sweaters and sweatshirts, wearing coats and scarves inside, and using a heated blanket.

Nicole: Usually I'm always cold, so I put on a lot of layers.

Jess: I try to wear a lot of sweaters, and we use blankets. I like to wear my coat around the house.

Carrie: We definitely put on clothing. Scarves, if needed. I think just this morning I was walking around with my scarf on because I was cold. You know, I've got my slippers, things like that.

Quinn: We also have a heated blanket which helps us keep the thermostat lower at night.

Orla: If he doesn't feel warm enough, he is more likely to hit the button and turn the heat up. I try not to do that. I would rather put on a sweater or drink warm drinks.

Owen: That is your cheapness coming out.

The degree to which my informants relied on these types of actions depended on their priorities, their expectations for how warm they should feel inside, and the extent to which members of a couple disagreed about what temperature they should keep their homes. Households who were very concerned with waste and their impacts on nature tended to rely more on interventions like putting on more clothes or sitting under a blanket, while households who were most worried about personal health and community concerns were generally less worried about saving energy. Indeed, my health-oriented informant Heather told me that saving energy was something that had not really occurred to her.

Comfort when it's warm outside

Temperatures

The indoor temperatures my informants prefer during hot weather varied considerably, from Scott and Sarah and Mike and Mina, who all recently relocated to Portland from California and run their air conditioner at 70 degrees Fahrenheit (21.1 degrees Celsius) all summer, to Gloria who recently relocated from the Midwest and says the indoor temperature that triggers her to turn on an air conditioner is "94 degrees (Fahrenheit, or

34.4 degrees Celsius) inside at night." While not all of my informants have space-cooling equipment, nearly all of my informants who do expressed a belief that the equipment should be used as little as possible and only when the indoor temperature is unbearable, even if their preference would be a lower indoor temperature.

Chris: In the summer, I think we tend to set it more for 78–80 [degrees Fahrenheit, or 25.6–26.7 degrees Celsius], and sometimes lower. But usually it's not that bad in Portland, or it hadn't been. I think I prefer it to be more like 75 [degrees Fahrenheit, or 23.9 degrees Celsius], but I would never set the air conditioner to that because that would make me want to punch myself in the face.

Emily: My goal is to set it at 78 [degrees Fahrenheit, or 25.6 degrees Celsius]. Which feels pretty nice on a 100-degree [Fahrenheit, or 37.8 degrees Celsius] day. But I work from home, but if I'm just sweating, I have to tap it down. But I try to *never* go below 72 [degrees Fahrenheit, or 22.2 degrees Celsius]. That's my floor.

Kirstin: Why do you have that as a floor?

Emily: It's random. It just feels like you shouldn't need it to be any cooler than that when it's like 100 [degrees Fahrenheit, or 37.8 degrees Celsius] out. 72 [degrees Fahrenheit, or 22.2 degrees Celsius] is pretty nice. And you just dress appropriately and drink ice water.

Brian: On the cooling side, I don't turn on air conditioning until I absolutely *have* to.

Kirstin: Do you have central air or window units?

Brian: I do have central air, and it's a heat pump with air conditioner. I think that it got to the high 90s [36–37 degrees Celsius] before I finally turned on the air conditioning last year.

There appears to be a moral dimension for many informants associated with using air-conditioning equipment during hot weather, and they had trouble explaining where these seemingly arbitrary boundaries come from.

Penny's home has central air conditioning, but she sets it to 78 degrees Fahrenheit (25.6 degrees Celsius), mostly for her pets. Nicole also thinks about her pets when she turns on the air conditioning.

Nicole: I actually hate AC, and I am more willing to let it get up to around 78. And we have five long-haired dogs, and so I'll turn it on if it looks like they are getting uncomfortable.

Both Penny and Nicole would prefer to use passive cooling techniques. Eric, too, prefers to sacrifice a couple of degrees and deal with his home being hotter so that he can use his passive cooling routine rather than run the central air conditioning in his home. Informants without cooling equipment are somewhat at the mercy of the weather when it comes to their indoor air temperature, but they also have ways of keeping it cool inside or ways to avoid being inside altogether.

Equipment

Most, but not all, of my informants had either central air or at least one window air-conditioning unit, while others used floor fans and ceiling fans. Andrew bought sun sails (a type of large fabric shade), planted a tree, and planted hops to help block the direct sun that heats his house, and Mike and Mina put up blinds. Scott and Sarah said they were thinking about getting some kind of window coverings because the direct sunlight meant that keeping their home cool, even with their central air conditioning, was a challenge.

Kyle and Kelly installed ceiling fans, and have one window air-conditioning unit for their young child. Several of my informants purchased air-conditioning units for their children or during pregnancy.

Kyle: We have one window AC unit for our kid's room. She's up on the third floor and it gets *really* hot. She goes to bed when the sun is still blasting into her room.

Ivy: Getting the window AC unit was motivated by having a baby and making sure her room wasn't 100 degrees [Fahrenheit, or 37.8 degrees Celsius].

In a moment of desperation, Wendy bought a window air-conditioning unit because she was so uncomfortable the summer she was pregnant, but she returned it to the store without opening it. Jim nearly bought a window unit when his child was an infant, but the temperature cooled off before he went through with the purchase. Both Wendy and Jim recounted these stories of nearly going through with adding indoor cooling equipment to their homes in a desperate moment with guilt, shame, and finally relief and pride that they didn't actually make the purchases.

Air conditioning is also described as being important for the evenings and for helping my informants get comfortable enough to sleep at night.

Heather: We don't have central cooling, we only have central heating. Once it gets hot out, we put window units only in our bedrooms. Neither of us can sleep when it's hot. We both like it cold when we're sleeping.

Brian: I usually end up with a week or more where air conditioning's on if I'm in the house in the evening because it's too uncomfortable otherwise.

Several households mention "breaking down" and buying window air conditioning during a very hot summer in Portland two years earlier. A single, very hot year can have a lasting impact on energy consumption and the ways that people stay comfortable inside when it's hot out.

Tim: We used to be able to get by just by opening the windows and closing the blinds and having that routine, but it seems like summers have been more severe the past few years. We just gave in and bought a portable AC two years ago. We needed a few nights of good sleep where we could get the air cool enough so we weren't dying.

Now that they have the air-conditioning equipment, they use it during the summer even though Tim had lived in Portland for over 15 years with no air conditioning. A single, very hot summer has permanently altered Tim and Tara's demand for energy.

Despite owning the air-conditioning unit, Tim prefers not to use it because he doesn't like the way refrigerated air feels. Several informants mentioned they would prefer to be slightly hotter inside and rely on electric fans and open windows to move the air around.

Tim: I would prefer having two fans instead and being able to feel air moving. I don't like AC air at all.

Emily: At night when he comes home, he's more often the one who's like, "Let's turn off the AC and open up the windows!" And I'm like, "Uuuuugh. It's still 88 degrees [Fahrenheit, or 31.1 degrees Celsius] out!" We get like two weeks of summer that's like that. But.

Eric: And I'd say my motivation for doing that is like half-financial, half that I just like feeling air movement, so that's just my preference even if we give up a couple degrees to get that.

Quinn: I grew up in the south, and we didn't have central air. I was used to just having fans so I'm comfortable with that. I put large window fans in the windows at night and get the breeze coming in. I don't put down blinds because the cats like to be in the sun, so I think about that.

Jim and Jess and Andrew and Amy replaced old windows in their homes that were permanently stuck shut to allow for more passive cooling.

Jess: We insulated this house, and we replaced the windows so they can open. And that makes a huge difference. And we have a ceiling fan in our room.

This is a substantial investment, but it allows these households to avoid relying on more energy-intensive ways of cooling the air.

Actions

While recent transplants from California Mike and Mina and Scott and Sarah were unapologetic about their air-conditioning use, most of my informants told me they try to use their air conditioning as sparingly as possible. They rely on other ways to stay comfortable when it's hot out, though they believe very hot weather is increasingly common during Portland summers.

Passive cooling rituals involving fans, blinds, and opening and closing windows were the most common way, other than air conditioning, to keep indoor spaces comfortable during hot weather.

Rob: I have my own pseudoscience way of arranging the fans that makes me believe it is creating an optimal airflow. I won't open the front windows for security reasons. We point the fans to point the fans in, and I've always wondered if it's better to blow the air in or out. And then I have another fan that I position at the bottom of the staircase to circulate the air upstairs.

Eric: When you live in the Central Valley [of California], you learn to have these routines. In the morning you open everything up. And then you're watching the temperature, and then you close everything, turn it [the air conditioning] on, and then as soon as you can … Just because one, because of how extreme the heat is during the summer, and two because electrical bills are so much more expensive.

Fiona: I keep my shades down when it's hot out, for sure. That's something that I learned from my mom's house where my stepdad would get up early on hot days and crack all the windows, and put all the blinds up for two hours to cool it off. And then as soon as it started getting hot put all the blinds down and close all the windows.

Kirstin: So he had like a whole routine?

Fiona: [laughing] He has a system.

Kirstin:	So do you follow his whole system, or have you just taken a piece of his system?
Fiona:	I pretty much do exactly that. I'll crack the windows, and turn the blinds down all day and leave them open all night so it cools off during the night.
Kyle:	My friend is from the south and spent a lot of years there as a working-class person, and he had a lot of skills around keeping cool without air conditioning. We were fortunate to have that practical introduction to another way to do things.
Carrie:	Oh! And there is a whole routine that he did learn from his parents about windows and blinds and like keeping … you know we open up as soon as …
Chris:	[laughing]
Kirstin:	And who does those the window routine?
Carrie:	Well, you know we both participate [laughing] I'll participate in it.
Kirstin:	But you [looking at Chris] are the driver of this? Of passive heating and cooling?
Chris:	Yeah for sure.
Carrie:	But yeah, you know just open it up at whatever point at night that it gets cool enough, and keep them open until either we leave the house or the point that it gets warm enough, and then we close the windows, close the shades.
Chris:	Shut everything down.
Carrie:	It definitely helps.
Chris:	It makes a huge difference.

My informants generally told me that they learned their passive cooling techniques from someone who had developed a "system" or "routine," often a parent or a roommate. Often, informants told me about these routines with a self-conscious laugh.

| Owen: | A number of years here, we had a window AC unit but we didn't really want to run them so we'd put fans in the windows. We learned that from her dad. |

When Owen and Orla had window air-conditioning units, they tried to use them very sparingly and relied instead on the passive cooling techniques they learned from Orla's father. Now that they replaced their oil furnace with a heat pump, they rely on the air-conditioning function of the heat pump more frequently. Replacing old furnaces with more efficient heat pumps may inadvertently increase overall energy demand, shifted between seasons, by creating summer space-cooling demand where there was none before. Once the new appliance is in place, people take advantage of the space-cooling function even if they installed the heat pump primarily for its space-heating capability.

Other actions my informants take involve moving to a cooler part of the home, leaving the home, playing in water, eating popsicles, drinking cool drinks, putting cold wet or frozen towels on, or sitting on blocks of ice.

Kyle: When it's hot out we use fans and go to the river. Try to leave. Splash pads in the parks downtown. We have heat-trapping blinds and open all of the windows at night.

Fiona: In Oregon, I feel like there are two days a year when air conditioning might be useful, but instead we go to the river or eat popsicles. Cold showers if we're not able to go somewhere.

Penny: When it's hot out, we have fans. We go swimming. Go get wet somewhere.

Carrie: Our basement is really comfortable in the summer.

Chris: Yeah we would go down there because it stays really cool down in the basement.

These techniques bring to mind the suggestion of Strengers (2012) to think outside the home and its "material infrastructure" to truly change the demand for electricity. My informants have changed the meaning of comfort when it's hot outside from a matter of achieving a particular indoor air temperature to interventions that frequently involve cooling their bodies directly with cold or frozen items, moving to a different part of the home, or leaving the home altogether.

Conclusion

Mary Douglas (2003 [1966], 2) writes that, "There is no such thing as absolute dirt: it exists in the eye of the beholder." The same might be said for comfort temperatures, which are at once formed socially and culturally, as well as based on individual tolerance and preference. So while Shove (2003) points out that the social meanings of cleanliness and comfort and the things we do to feel clean and comfortable have changed in ways that place increasing demands on natural resources, my informants reveal the potential reductions in demand for resources associated with changing the social meanings of cleanliness and comfort, and, with that, the accompanying time and resource-demanding practices. Learning to accept being a little bit dirtier saves both time and money. Cohabitating people with different preferences and practices related to cleanliness and indoor comfort may find themselves in conflict—the subject of Chapter 8. A consistent theme across the discussions with my informants about their cleanliness and comfort temperature practices was the importance of learning new practices or returning to old ones that had been previously abandoned in their efforts to get things done in everyday life in ways that feel consistent with their environmental priorities. In Chapter 7, I will explore this theme in more detail—what role do learning and research play in discontinuing conventional ways of getting things done and adopting more environmentally friendly practices? As with many aspects of daily life in these households, the results are contradictory, frequently frustrating, and rarely straightforward or easy.

References

Bushman, Richard L. and Claudia L. Bushman (1988) "The early history of cleanliness in America," *Journal of American History*, 74(4): 1213–1238.

Cowan, Ruth Schwarz (1983) *More Work for Mother: The Ironies of Household Technologies from the Open Hearth to the Microwave*, New York: Basic Books.

Douglas, Mary (2003 [1966]) *Purity and Danger: An Analysis of Concepts of Pollution and Taboo*, London: Routledge.

Hoy, Suellen (1996) *Chasing Dirt: The American Pursuit of Cleanliness*, Oxford: Oxford University Press.

Lynd, Robert S. and Helen Merrell Lynd (1929) *Middletown: A Study in American Culture*, San Diego, CA: Harcourt Brace Jovanovich.

Parr, Joy (1997) "What makes washday less blue? Gender, nation, and technology choice in postwar Canada," *Technology and Culture*, 38(1): 153–186.

Project Laundry List (2013) "Laundry Fact Sheet," Available: http://www.laundrylist.org/wp-content/uploads/2013/08/facts.pdf [Accessed June 22, 2017].

Rilke, Rainer Maria (1969) *Letters of Rainer Maria Rilke, 1892–1910*. Translated by Jane Bannard Greene and M.D. Herter Norton. New York: W.W. Norton.

Shove, Elizabeth (2003) *Comfort, Cleanliness, and Convenience: The Social Organization of Normality*, Oxford: Berg.

Shove, Elizabeth (2004) "Sustainability, system innovation and the laundry," in Boelie Elzen, Frank W. Geels, and Kenneth Green (eds) *System Innovation and the Transition to Sustainability: Theory, Evidence and Policy*, Cheltenham: Edward Elgar Publishing, pp 76–94.

Strengers, Yolande (2012) "Peak electricity demand and social practice theories: Reframing the role of change agents in the energy sector," *Energy Policy*, 44: 226–234.

U.K. Office for National Statistics (2011) "Living Costs and Food Survey," Available: http://www.ons.gov.uk/ons/rel/family-spending/family-spending/family-spending-2011-edition/consumer-durables-nugget.xls [Accessed June 22, 2017].

U.S. Bureau of Labor Statistics (2016) "American Time Use Survey: Chart 15," Available: https://www.bls.gov/tus/charts/chart15.txt [Accessed June 22, 2017].

U.S. Energy Information Administration (2013) "2009 Residential Energy Consumption Survey: Table HC3.1 Appliances in U.S. Homes, by Housing Unit Type, 2009," Available: https://www.eia.gov/consumption/resident ial/data/2009/hc/hc3.1.xls [Accessed June 22, 2017].

Watson, Sophie (2015) "Mundane objects in the city: Laundry practices and the making and remaking of public/private sociality and space in London and New York," *Urban Studies*, 52(5): 876–890.

7

Doing Their Own Research

Kirstin: Can you describe a family that you know where you're
             like, "I am not like that, and I don't want to be like that?"
Heather: That's easy! Someone who doesn't do their own
             research. Followers.

None of my informants grew up exactly the same way that they live now,
so many of them had to spend considerable amounts of time and effort
to learn about sustainability and new sustainable ways of getting things
done in everyday life. They talk to friends and family members, they read
books and websites, and they learn on the job as part of their waged work
to gain practical know-how and to acquire information that helps them
make more environmental choices. These efforts might be called "human
capital acquisition" in the jargon of neoclassical economics—investments in
productivity-enhancing skills that involved a trade-off to acquire. In other
words, my informants' research represents time—and in some cases, also
money—that could have been used for some other purpose but that was
dedicated to gaining skills and knowledge. Or, these efforts might be seen as
gaining "competence" in theories of social practice—"which encompasses
skill, know-how, and technique" (Shove, Pantzar, & Watson 2012, 14). And
these efforts to acquire know-how that is useful for bringing everyday life
into alignment with pro-environmental values can be thought of as one
component of the unwaged work that takes place in these eco-conscious
households—an input into the household production process.

In the time since these interviews were conducted, the concept of "doing
one's own research" became associated during the COVID-19 pandemic
with skeptics organizing anti-mask rallies, refusing vaccines, and taking
unproven treatments or preventatives such as medications formulated for
livestock. The phrase now appears with the word "research" in quotation
marks in internet memes, such as "2021: I did my own 'research'" engraved
on a gravestone, or "You keep using this word 'research.' I don't think it
means what you think it means," featuring a photo of Mandy Patinkin as

Inigo Montoya from the 1987 movie *The Princess Bride*. Today, "doing one's own research" is a position that is contrasted unfavorably by critics of these conspiracy theorists with scientists who do "real" research.

Many of my informants do not see "science" as neutral, and they do not trust the government, scientists, or the medical establishment to produce research or recommendations that promote environmental preservation or the safety of their families. Yvonne explained:

> I feel that from my research and what I just hear on a day-to-day basis is that the main concern for corporations is just the bottom line— money. I just see and hear and read so much about all of the horrible aftermath of a company's decision to just go ahead and put something out into the world without really either researching it or caring if they knew that it wasn't a safe product. So I do not trust companies because I just I don't trust capitalism … in the sense of caring about everyday regular people. I don't think that they care about us in any way shape or form. And why would they, if it's cheaper not to?

For these informants, mainstream scientific and medical knowledge production can be influenced by corporate interests and is not always consistent with my informants' environmental values. Jennifer Reich (2014) argues that mothers who subscribe to ideas related to natural living and maternal choice with respect to routine childhood immunizations have internalized neoliberal ideologies related to personal responsibility and individual choice. These mothers "conduct research, largely from sources they view as independent from healthcare professionals and, thus, more credible" (Reich 2014, 688). For the mostly affluent and White mothers in Reich's sample, the availability of these choices is "facilitated by access to resources" (Reich 2014, 682). However, these mothers negatively judge others because "neoliberalism … masks how access to privilege makes choice possible" (Reich 2014, 684). While this may be true for some of my more health-oriented informants—for example Heather—I believe there is another way to explain the motivations behind my more diverse sample of informants and their research. Rather than having internalized the neoliberal ideology of individual choice and personal responsibility, I believe my informants are coping with the consequences of neoliberalism (Tanir 2020)—a shrinking welfare state, costly and inaccessible healthcare, declining budgets for scientific research, and corporate lobbyists influencing government decisions to prioritize profits over environmental safety and public health.

"Doing their own research" changes the way sustainability-oriented households get things done because it gives them information about their choices or makes them better (or more efficient) at certain practices.

Research and knowledge about some sustainable household practices might also make people more efficient in waged employment—a substitute for other types of human capital. Or knowledge gained on the job in waged employment might make people more efficient at household sustainability practices. In some cases, the people I spoke with had to learn for themselves to care about sustainability issues, since this was not a priority in the households or communities they grew up in, and then had to learn new practices to bring their lifestyles into harmony with their values. While some of my informants learned about environmental issues like littering as children from television commercials or in school, as adults they have some skepticism about those messages, as I discuss in more detail in Chapter 5. People raised in families with ties to environmentalism or other countercultural movements may have absorbed some of their current priorities and practices from their parents, but adaptation occurs—to an urban setting, to account for contemporary climate change or health considerations, to incorporate new information about the relative impact of choices, or to a household with two working parents.

Household research topics were varied, but most often included research into health information, skills and how to do things, and information about the environmental impact of household choices. My informants were motivated to conduct this research because of a general lack of trust in institutions and the government, as well as a desire for self-sufficiency. They do not feel that they can rely on the state, corporations, or other "mainstream" institutions to operate with their priorities or best interests in mind, so they must take matters into their own hands when it comes to health and the environment.

Learning skills

Because few of my informants grew up in highly ecologically conscious households, they needed to learn ways of getting things done that differ from the ways they were raised and their parents got things done. Their late teens and early 20s were an important life phase when my informants were frequently exposed to new ideas and learned new habits, such as selective flushing and preparing and eating fresh foods. Other informants, such as Mina who recently relocated from Los Angeles, told me that moving to Portland and being exposed to people getting things done more sustainably was a big influence, prompting them to adopt practices that might have been unthinkable in their previous locations.

Mina: This is stuff that I am more interested in since moving here because the current groups I find myself in have influenced me. Down in California, it would have taken me a long time

to find these things. Friends and people I've met here have
had a huge influence.

Still, it is important to my informants to make these practices and skills
their own.

Heather: We know a family who are doing a sort of *Into the Wild* thing.
           Her husband lived in complete nature for 20 years where he
           lived off the land. And that is amazing, but that is not us. And
           he has lots of skills to teach us, which I think are important
           for us to get back to our roots, but integrating them into
           our lifestyle.

After her family's recent move to Portland, Heather has encountered other
highly sustainability-oriented families, some with practices that are more
extreme than the ones she chooses to adopt. Finding balance is important
for her household, who are not explicitly opposed to living in "civilization."
    The Internet also plays a large role in learning new skills and practices. To
learn how to fix her broken furnace, Penny relied on online tutorials and
instructional videos, which saved her money and gave her a sense of pride
in accomplishing the repair herself. Fiona was able to learn how to make
her own cloth diapers out of unwanted clothes from instructional websites
before she had access to a low-income cloth diaper rental program, and
later funds from her Earned Income Tax Credit. Mina relies on blogs about
natural parenting and eco-conscious alternatives to conventional ways of
getting things done.

Mina: When I am looking for people who are promoting a more
           environmentally conscious way of life, what I find is a lot
           of people who don't trust vaccines, or think other medical
           things are also bad. For example, *Wellness Mama* [website].
           She's got a ton of information for nettle tea, and essential
           oils, and making your own this or that. She has recipes for
           everything, and she has like six kids, *and* she homeschools.
           It's bananas. But I remember how she handles her children's
           colds. She gives them Vitamin C on the hour every hour,
           and I'm thinking, "Oh my gosh. Who has the time?"

While she finds some of the information about skills useful, there are
other elements about the websites and blogs that she doesn't like, such as
promoting antivaccine views and types of intensive mothering that she views
as "bananas." She no longer uses the social network Facebook because she
found the communities for alternative parenting similarly too intense.

A disproportionate number of informants in my sample have waged work in what might be called the "sustainability industrial complex"—as educators in environmental fields, in environmental nonprofits, or in small sustainability-oriented businesses. This is at least in part due to the generally anti-corporate values of my informants, who want to work in jobs and industries that reflect their values.

Kyle: I've never worked in the for-profit sector. I worked in the government sector, and I was a consultant to nonprofits and worked for nonprofits. So I've always stayed away from organizations whose values I can't get on board with.

Penny: I find myself drawn to positions that have an outreach or education component. So even if I'm not physically saving the world, at least I'm sending people out in the world with more knowledge. I've looked at data analysis jobs and stuff like that, and I think it would make me unhappy. I could never take a job if it was doing something to harm the environment or people.

But another possible explanation is that an information or competence feedback loop between waged work in the sustainability sector and unwaged sustainability production in the home means that there is substitutability for the know-how (or human capital) involved in both waged and unwaged sustainability work, as I discussed in Chapter 4. Skills that are desirable or useful for waged work in a sustainability-oriented job might also make someone more efficient in their unwaged work in sustainability-oriented household production.

Carrie: Through his job, he [Chris] learns about the stuff and we take advantage of certain opportunities, so it's definitely influential just knowing what exists and how to do things.

Dayna learned about recycling from *Master Recyclers* at her office, coworkers who have taken a free course sponsored by local governments and the Oregon Department of Environmental Quality, who then share information about recycling best practices in the workplace as volunteer trained recycling experts. The organization where Dayna works also sponsors lunchtime seminars with speakers on sustainability topics.

Dayna: Learning about things occasionally deeply influences my thinking. Maybe that's going to happen with me with cosmetics and body stuff when I learn more about that. I'm not a cosmetics and like body products person but I'm afraid learning more is going to ruin them for me.

She brings what she learns home and implements changes to the way she gets things done, most recently by deciding to eat less red meat because of the carbon impacts of beef production.

But this substitutability between the types of know-how that are helpful for sustainable household production and those that are helpful for waged work in a sustainability-oriented job goes both ways—skills that are useful for unwaged work in sustainability-oriented household production might also be desirable skills for waged work in the sustainability industry. David's education and training is in the health field, but he now works at an environmental nonprofit after his involvement in making major energy-efficiency improvements to his home during a gut remodel. His skills and know-how related to ecologically conscious household production were useful for his new career in the sustainability industrial complex. Heather uses her skills related to household production and natural mothering to sell essential oils through a multilevel marketing business, and Fiona now works in a preschool where she uses the skills she learned as a mother. Investments in know-how related to household production can pay off in waged work, too. In each of these cases, there is an additional feedback loop: at these jobs, my informants gain more know-how which influences their household practices and choices.

Types of research

These eco-conscious households try to get information about health practices, the health and safety of consumer goods, and about the environmental impact of their choices. They feel they can't trust consumer goods or medical treatments to be safe, they feel a sense of personal responsibility for climate change mitigation, and they believe governments aren't regulating companies sufficiently to ensure environmental preservation. This means that the task of learning about sustainability and sustainability practices falls to people like my respondents. When my informants talk about "doing their own research," for the most part they mean reading books and websites and talking to friends and family members. Victor's research was more literal—when he was unable to find the exact health information that he was looking for, he started conducting medical experiments on his family with various supplements, measuring the results with blood tests, and posting the results online on a blog.

Health research

Research was particularly important for families with a strong personal health priority. Most often, they rely on internet sources like natural parenting blogs or the Environmental Working Group website for information on the safety of medical interventions, food, and personal care products. Emily describes herself as an anxious person, and since becoming a parent, a lot of her anxiety is directed toward making choices for her children:

Emily: I think there are a lot of things that are stressful about parenting. You worry that they're going to get hit by a car. You worry about pretty much everything. Are they developing right? Does my kid have autism? There's a million and five things to worry about.

Emily's personality and background in environmental science also make her a fastidious researcher of her family's heath choices. She reads websites run by organizations like the Environmental Working Group to learn about chemicals and contaminants in consumer goods.

Emily: Every decision that I make, especially around the parenting arena, is really tortuously considered. Looking up information, and looking up pros and cons of circumcision, vaccination, food, is it worth it to pay extra for this organic food? And I look up the Dirty Dozen, and I think, OK well, we definitely have to buy strawberries and apples and broccoli organic, but avocados we don't have to buy those organic. Like very, very careful but I approach it [sustainability] more from a health standpoint.

This practice of researching health and nutrition choices predates her children, and started when she realized she had some food intolerances, but she brings a scientific approach to her research habits.

Emily: I have been kind of like a hobby nutritional researcher. I was always doing it, even before becoming a parent. Just trying to weed through conflicting messaging and trying to land in a place where I feel good. For example, reading both sides of is it good to eat dairy or not.

Yvonne's interest in herbalism and making her own herbal medicines for her family came about when her son was diagnosed with asthma and she found her pediatrician was unable to answer her questions about the safety of his medications in a way that satisfied her or made her feel confident in the care her son was receiving.

Yvonne: My son was diagnosed with asthma and got really sick. He didn't almost die or anything, but he got really, really sick when he was about four. He was put on steroids and it just didn't make me feel comfortable that he was on steroids every day. I just I didn't like the lack of information on long-term use of steroids in children. So I started talking to naturopaths, and I started doing my own research into what could help him. I've always been interested in alternative medicine, but that experience was probably the moment where I started doing my own research and making my own medicines.

Heather's education and career as a nurse also influence her approach to researching the health choices she makes for her family. She is very critical of conventional medicine, conventionally grown food, and conventional cleaning products. Like Emily, Heather uses the Environmental Working Group website as a source for information, but she also uses more alternative sources for information, such as the reading she did to support her initial opposition to water fluoridation and fluoride toothpaste.

Heather: I make my own laundry detergent, and we try to do that mindfully by using the Environmental Working Group website as a reference. Our environment in modern-day society has so many toxins. If I can provide my children something that is less toxic … my children are my motivation for all of this.

While Emily is sensitive to barriers related to socioeconomic class and education that may prevent people from doing the same type of research and making the same choices she makes for her family, Heather is critical of people who don't seek out non-mainstream heath alternatives:

Heather: So many people just go through parenthood without really making it something they need to look into and research. My younger sister just had a baby, and she just does mainstream without looking into it a little deeper.

For Heather, part of being a good parent is "looking into it a little deeper" and seeing and researching what she sees as healthier alternatives to conventional ways of getting things done. She is very strong in her belief that she is making the best choices for her children, and it seems to disappoint her that more people don't share her priorities and practices.

One of the problems with research into chemicals and toxins and contamination is that there is no way to eliminate all possibility of contamination. Indeed, some informants are unconvinced of the benefits of exhaustive health research into what their children are eating and doing.

Brian: I'm more skeptical of health claims than other parents, I think. There's this kind of unavoidable pressure on parenting that is always on doing parenting a little bit better, which I try to avoid. And to the Nth degree. It just gets ridiculous. People get more and more obsessive about "I'm exposing my child to some risk of injury," or whatever else. And I think that in Portland, or in similar cities across the country, I think that there is an "Are you giving food that might give your kid some exposure to some ingredient that they might possibly form an allergy to?" Or that [laughing] or is maybe possibly dangerous to them? And I'm pretty sensitive to that stuff. And I do think there are ingredients that are dangerous. And I do think there are things in our food system that are a real freaking mess, but ... Parenting has become kind of a high-stakes thing.

Brian loves his child dearly and cares about his well-being. He also acknowledges a lack of appropriate health and safety regulation of food and other industries in the United States. Given these realities, there is no end to the amount of research a person could do.

Research about the environmental impact of choices

For my informants whose sustainability practices are motivated by an interest in environmental preservation, conducting research into the relative environmental impacts of practices is an important aspect of household decision-making. Dayna and David rely on friends and coworkers whom they trust. Since these personal contacts have similar values and have already done this research, David and Dayna feel comfortable following their advice. Penny and Ivy like to talk to the employees of a local for-profit recycling center to learn more about how to properly sort and recycle their household waste that isn't accepted for curbside recycling. Penny has also done additional research online about recycling to learn where the materials are sent and how they are processed. Wendy and her wife read books to find out the relative carbon/environmental impact of choices, something that is particularly important to Wendy's wife. Rebecca did research online to find out about the relative impacts of cloth and disposable diapers.

Rebecca: We use cloth diapers and we use a local diaper service. And I did research and I don't think it is more sustainable than disposable because of the amount of hot water that you need to use to launder them.

Her household uses both disposable and cloth diapers, but she is not convinced that the cloth diapers are obviously more sustainable than disposable diapers because the process of washing them is also resource-intensive.

Jim came to similar conclusions about cloth diapering, though he and Jess did use cloth diapers for their child after doing extensive research into the relative environmental impacts of cloth and disposable diapers. He still feels bad about having made the wrong environmental choice, and he feels frustrated about not having access to definitive information about the relative impacts of his choices. In addition to the diapers, he told me about researching the carbon impacts of food, travel, clothing, bed linens, heating using the home's furnace versus the fireplace, and whether to buy a new car or keep his household's old one.

Jim: I struggle with where to find information. Not just with food but with all environmental choices. I've read quite a few books, and some are better than others. A book that was helpful was *How Bad are Bananas?* It tries to establish a carbon impact of food and other lifestyle choices. A lot of it is estimates, which gives you a good starting point. It's super important and also nearly impossible to get accurate information about the relative carbon impacts of different choices.

He relies on books and websites, but finds the lack of clear information unsatisfying and vexing.

Jim: I enjoy talking about our environmental choices with Jess, I enjoy researching it, but I find it frustrating that I can't find information that I trust. A lot of the decisions or nondecisions that we make are because we just don't know what the right thing to do is.

Jim wants to make the right choices for the environment, but the information he would need to make all of the right choices is rarely clear, when it is even available.

Motivations for research

Regardless of the informant's particular combination of priorities in the sustainability realm, their research is largely inspired by two motivations that are often seen by my informants as inextricably linked—the protection of the environment and the health of household members. They believe protection of the environment and the health of their household members have become their responsibility. Each household does this research and modifies their practices because they don't trust other institutions, such as the government or corporations, to take action against these potential harms on a larger scale. Because my informants feel that they can't trust institutions to make decisions that reflect their sustainability values, many of the households I spoke with value self-sufficiency as a way of getting things done.

Particularly for informants with a strong health priority, an interest in sustainability grew out of a lack of trust in Western medicine. Beyond health and medicine, my informants do not trust that products available to consumers will be safe and that the government will adequately regulate corporations.

Heather: Families who solely trust the system are not us.
Emily: The FDA [Food and Drug Administration] or the USDA [United States Department of Agriculture] approves chemicals because they haven't been proven to be *unsafe*. But nobody's proven that they're safe. Where's the 30-year study on Roundup? And who is doing the study? And are they being paid by Monsanto?

Because they can't trust the government and the companies that produce and sell products to prioritize their health and that of their children, my informants must do this research for themselves. Those informants who see the protection of the environment as their personal responsibility must do research to learn about environmental impact-minimizing practices because they don't believe appropriate actions to mitigate climate change and other environmental and social problems are being taken by the government or large corporations. Informants like Jim and Nathan also don't trust other people who see themselves as sustainability-oriented to make evidence-based choices that are actually good for the environment; as a result, these informants are skeptical of labels like "organic" and "environmentalist."

Jim: I am skeptical of calling ourselves "environmentalists" even though we strive to make the right environmental choices. We are always skeptical or realistic that we're doing enough. Whereas other people might recycle or buy a Prius and feel like they've solved the problem. We never feel like we are doing enough, and I never feel like I can solve any problem with choices I make in my lifestyle.
Nathan: I don't think there is any meaningful difference between organic and not. I don't think there is sufficient control over the concept of organic that I can understand it. I think a lot of that is a matter of marketing. I am actually pro-GMO [genetically modified organism] because I understand its

consequences in terms of energy efficiency in production. The farmer doesn't benefit much from the organic label, and it's really hard on him economically. Yes, your prices go up a little bit, and your costs go up exponentially.

My informants feel out of step with mainstream America, and many of them also feel like they have little in common with others who care about sustainability issues because of what they've learned from their extensive research and expertise on sustainability. While it is easy to care about the environment, it can be more difficult to actually follow through and make more drastic interventions into mundane practices.

Penny: I think there is a disconnect, and I don't know if it's because people just get too busy, but I know that a lot of people my age are big consumers. They might shop at New Seasons [natural food store] and buy all this organic food, but they're also buying tons of packaged food, and buying tons of new clothes constantly. They want to be doing the right thing, but they still want whatever they want. I'm not going to blame them for that, but I agonize over things.

A consequence of research for my informants is the guilt that accompanies the knowledge of just how bad many mundane practices are for the environment.
    While my informants may feel like their lives are very different from more conventional Americans, many of them share a very American value that motivates much of their research and many of their practices: a desire for self-sufficiency.

Dayna: Self-sufficiency or self-reliance is something that is a theme for a lot of the decisions that we make.

Learning ways to be self-sufficient and finding information on sustainability practices related to self-sufficiency is an important type of research.

Gloria: I get information from the Internet, I get information from the library, and I get information from getting to know people who are already doing what I want to do. And then doing it myself and the trial and error, whether it's composting, or chickens, or the vegetable garden.
Ivy: I literally googled "things to think about when moving out of the city to the farm." And reading the blogs of people who have done that.

132

For Ivy, self-sufficiency is more aspirational than part of her current day-to-day reality, as she fantasizes about moving to a rural area. My informants who are passionate about self-sufficiency were never clear on why self-sufficiency is a good thing other than that it "feels good" or has some affective benefits. Self-sufficiency was seen as good for its own sake.

Ivy: If I wasn't working and I could just be a stay-at-home farm mom, I would be the happiest woman alive. I'd make EVERYTHING. My kid would be wearing all these crooked clothes and so would I! That's ideal! Being able to completely sustain yourself. Growing all your food … that's the Holy Grail. It's healthy and wholesome.

Some informants may see themselves and their practices as reflecting self-sufficiency, when many of their practices are enabled by government subsidies and tax benefits, such as Dayna's solar panels that she views as "generating our own electricity."

Dayna: I like that I feel that we are self-sufficient. The self-sufficiency aspect. The same way that it makes me feel good to be able to grow a portion of our own food. To be able to be generating our own electricity, that makes me feel really good. It's just damn satisfying, too.

Not all of my informants emphasized this idea of self-sufficiency and the affective benefits. Kyle, a socialist living in intentional community, believes that homesteading and self-sufficiency are not environmentally friendly ways to live.

Kyle: Homesteaders aspire to being on the land and out of a city. And in terms of my environmentalism, I have a practical mind and I believe the most efficient way to live is in an urban area. It involves less consumption. Rural living is just very carbon-intensive and the schlepping of stuff unless you are a survivalist. But that requires a very large tract of land per person.

Penny also felt good and empowered when she was able to fix her furnace with only the help of online tutorials. However, Penny believes in the importance of understanding the impact of her actions on others—near and far—and doesn't see living in isolation as a solution to environmental problems.

Gloria: The part of "off the grid" that doesn't sit well with me is the association that off the grid excludes community. "Off the grid" and community are mutually exclusive. You cannot live off the grid and have a community.

Gloria sees self-sufficiency practices like vegetable gardening and owning chickens as a solution to the high costs of local and organic produce, but sees living in isolation as antithetical to her sustainability priorities.

Research consequences

Households often had a particular family member with a designated researcher role. For Heather, this is due to differences in education between herself and her spouse, while for Emily, Jim, Mina, and Wendy this is more due to differences in personality and interests.

Heather: He is always on board. He knows I have all the right intentions and that I do all the right research. He knows that I have the background and the education. It's never an argument. He trusts me. And that's also true when it comes to parenting things like not "crying it out" and co-sleeping and stuff like that. He's the workhorse and I'm the mastermind.

Eric: I get the benefit from all the heavy thinking and research that Emily does. I would say that I'm a little bit more pragmatic. I won't do the exhaustive research. I am either following Emily's lead or I'm looking at the options that are available to me and just kind of making a quick instinctive decision—I think is the one that is the better option from an environmental perspective.

The "researcher" in the couple does the research, and the other member of the couple generally goes along with their ideas, or, in the case of Mike, mostly tolerates or ignores the sustainability practices and does his own thing.

Several informants told me that they believe more people would make these same choices and engage in similar sustainability practices if they were only exposed to the right information.

Gloria: If it was just loaded into your brain like Neo in *The Matrix*, the benefits, the costs of attachment parenting, and the drawbacks. The benefits, the costs of cry-it-out and the drawbacks. If people understood all of that, I think most people would make a different choice and choose the alternative way of doing things.

Tara, Fiona, and Eric see this access to information as a privilege, and feel grateful for their ability to understand research, to know where to find information, and for their ability to follow through and make changes to the way they get things done.

Tara: I think what would be hard about [not recycling] would be knowing the shame associated with not knowing any better. Maybe they haven't had anyone who taught them, and then they are feeling judged.

Fiona: I have a concern with being what I would call classist. What I am really trying to avoid is saying that people who choose those [sustainability] things are better. I just think that if you have the choice and the information and the resources that you would probably make those [sustainability] choices.

Eric: We feel fortunate that we're able to make some of the decisions that we are because of both education reasons and financial reasons. And recognize that we are more sustainable because we have those means available to us. And we are aware of that, and that allows us to be more sustainable than we otherwise would be.

These informants also share the view that people shouldn't be judged negatively who make different choices because they don't have access to the same information, education, or financial resources. In the view of these informants, it is not the fault of people who make different choices. Sustainability practices can be time-consuming or expensive, but, most of all, these alternative sustainable ways of getting things done can be difficult to learn about for people who are not regularly exposed to this kind of information or these kinds of practices. These informants were careful to not sound elitist or judgmental or classist—they see their ability to do research into alternative ways of getting things done and to understand sustainability information as forms of advantage they have over others.

Conclusion

At the end of the day, the reason my informants need to do this research at all is because they believe it is their personal responsibility to keep the environment and their families safe from potentially harmful industries and the impacts of pollution and chemicals. This notion of personal responsibility isn't the result of my informants having individually internalized neoliberal ideology, as Reich (2014) argues about her sample of "natural living"-inclined mothers, but rather this is the *consequence* of neoliberal policies, institutions, and transformations as Tanir (2020) argues.

Emily told me that the research about what is and isn't safe for her children just isn't being done either by governments or industry. In the rare cases when the research is being conducted, Emily doesn't trust the results. My informants need to learn new ways of getting things done in everyday life to bring their mundane practices into balance with their environmental priorities. They look at "mainstream America" and they don't like what they see. For this reason, many of my informants want to separate themselves from conventional U.S. society to create their own communities or to live in isolation from the aspects of contemporary life that they find distasteful or in conflict with their priorities. Other informants see a "back-to-the-land" or "off-the-grid" lifestyle as antithetical to sustainability. Somewhat ironically, this ethic of independence and self-sufficiency is at the core of mainstream American identity (Fineman 2000). Some of my informants, such as Eric, Fiona, and Tara, believe that people who don't have access to good information about sustainability practices shouldn't be judged negatively, and that doing so may be elitist or classist. However, for other informants, "doing your own research" because you don't trust generally available information or mainstream practices means you are not, as Heather puts it, one of the "followers."

References

Fineman, Martha Albertson (2000) "Cracking the foundational myths: Independence, autonomy, and self-sufficiency," *Journal of Gender, Social Policy & the Law*, 8(15): 13–29.

Reich, Jennifer A. (2014) "Neoliberal mothering and vaccine refusal: Imagined gated communities and the privilege of choice," *Gender & Society*, 28(5): 679–704.

Shove, Elizabeth, Mika Pantzar, and Matt Watson (2012) *The Dynamics of Social Practice: Everyday Life and How It Changes*, London: SAGE.

Tanir, Canan (2020) "To Whom Does the Natural Come Naturally? Neoliberal Ideals of Motherhood in Turkey," Proquest Dissertations Publishing.

8

Conflict

Conflicts due to differences in preferences, priorities, and the social meanings associated with mundane practices within households are the premise of countless television sitcoms—between parents and their adult children in *Absolutely Fabulous, Frasier,* and *Steptoe and Son*; between parents and their children in *The Simpsons, Family Ties, Out of this World,* and *King of the Hill*; between spouses in *Bewitched, I Love Lucy, Dharma & Greg,* and *Keeping up Appearances*; between nonrelated adults living together, as in *Mr. Belvedere, The Nanny, Who's the Boss, Father Ted,* and *Perfect Strangers*. In each of these cases, these differences are exploited for comedic effect. In the 1963 *Steptoe and Son* episode "The Bath," the more fastidious and forward-looking adult son Harold explains to his rag-and-bone-man father Albert—who seems trapped in the late 19th century—that their current arrangement of bathing infrequently in a metal basin in the front room is no longer acceptable: "A lot of people don't live like that anymore … Those days is gone. It's a social stigma these days. You might as well have a horse sitting in the armchair and be done with it." Harold interprets his father's bathing practices as acts of "extreme dirtiness"—a meaning not shared by Albert.

Each of the households I spoke with for this book have their own unique combinations of environmental priorities, resources, and constraints—described in detail in Chapters 3 and 4—and conflict often arises both within and across households when these differences clash and compromise proves difficult. Chasms between the social meaning of practices can be too large to cross, particularly for these household members who are outside the "mainstream" and for whom the environmental stakes of mundane practices feel high. My informants often laughed—sometimes nervously—when they revealed these conflicts to me. While these sorts of interpersonal conflicts were generally conveyed in a lighthearted and affectionate manner, these differences are a real source of tension and stress, and at times have the potential to harm household members' physical or emotional well-being.

Interpersonal conflict in households where priorities and the social meaning of practices clash is relatable—this is perhaps why these culture clashes and fish-out-of-water household scenarios are such persistent themes in television sitcoms. This conflict comes into sharp relief in this set of households who have made deliberate and sometimes quite drastic interventions in mundane practices to pursue environmental priorities. What we see is an already universally fraught situation—unique human beings cohabitating and disagreeing—exacerbated by unconventional, often time-consuming practices and heartfelt passion for environmental priorities. This chapter explores how these differences in priorities and the social meaning of practices in eco-conscious households produce conflict within these households and the close personal relationships of household members.

My informants see their practices and priorities as unconventional, and many have made deliberate choices to distance themselves from mainstream U.S. values and ways of getting things done. A consequence is that these households sometimes come into conflict with others who do not share their priorities and practices. Within individual households, there tended to be differences between the adults in their sustainability priorities—either one adult will be more committed to alternative ways of getting things done, or adults will have different priorities in the sustainability realm. There are also differences in the meanings that household members ascribe to practices. Differences in the priorities and practices of my adult informants and their own parents also provoked conflicts, some minor and some more relationship-altering. While never framed as an outright conflict between parents and children, my informants were working actively to teach their children to adopt practices that matched their household's sustainability priorities. These lessons often emerged when children were doing something my informants deemed wasteful. My informants acknowledged that their unconventional practices and priorities may result in conflicts between their children and conventional elements of the world outside their household. Finally, my informants discussed internal struggles and guilt associated with making choices for pragmatic reasons that are not aligned with their sustainability priorities.

Conflicts between adult household members

Many of the couples I spoke with began their relationships on the basis of their shared values and priorities or developed these sustainability views and habits over the course of their relationship together. In other couples, such as Mike and Mina, sustainability is a newer interest that is not shared. Some informants also currently live with nonrelated adults—like Leonda, who lives with their partner and a roommate, and Kyle and Kelly, who live with Kelly's mother and another nuclear family in a small intentional community. Many of my informants learned some of their current household practices from previous roommates with whom they'd come into conflict. Conflicts over sustainability practices arise between adults when they have different sustainability priorities, when they share priorities but have different beliefs and information, when their priorities are held with different levels of intensity, or when one partner is the sole member of the household driving the sustainability priorities and efforts.

One way that conflicts between adults can arise is when a couple who shares sustainability *priorities* nonetheless has different beliefs and knowledge about sustainability *practices*. Recycling was one of the areas where this conflict occurred fairly regularly in the households I spoke with. Portland has recycling rules that have changed over time and that my informants find are not always intuitive. While recycling was a universal practice in the households I spoke with, household members had different levels of compliance with recycling rules. There was often a member of the couple who was the recycling expert and who worked to enforce recycling rules in the household. A conversation between Dayna and David about their different opinions on recycling brings this type of conflict into focus:

Dayna:	David goes based on the *spirit* of what he thinks *should* be recyclable. This is a big, long-term marital thing where David thinks that things he thinks he should be able to recycle at the curbside, if he puts it in the curbside recycling bin, even though it's not recyclable it's "sending a message" that they *should* be taking this thing. And I'm just like, you're making people's lives more difficult.
Kirstin:	So, David, you're laughing.
Dayna:	Because it's true!
David:	I mean, it's like … marginally true. I may have used to have done that.
Kirstin:	So what is something that you think should be recyclable that you have put in the recycling?
David:	Like clamshells, plastic clamshells. Those aren't supposed to go in the recycling, but I sneak those in there.
Dayna:	Mostly it's plastics, for David. A lot of plastics or to-go containers or wax …
David:	Dayna always tells me that the paper boxes that go in the freezer …
Dayna:	[shouting] ARE NOT RECYCLABLE!
David:	But they look like they should be recyclable and they have the recycling symbol on them …
Dayna:	So David puts them in there anyway! [shouting] And I'm like NO! You're not following the rules! The Master Recycler people have been very clear.

David: Even the ones with the little symbol on them? I mean, it
            looks like they're recyclable.
Dayna: NO. So ... [laughing]

David and Dayna are laughing to diffuse the tension of this part of our conversation, which had a definite sitcomesque flavor. As Dayna was talking, she was attempting to draw me in as an accomplice in her grievance, gesturing humorously and looking at me like a sitcom wife might look to the television camera to say to the audience at home, "Can you believe this guy?" There is an aspect of performance to the interviews I conducted, as my informants seek to paint a sympathetic picture about their lives in response to my questions. Dayna's voice conveyed real frustration as she told me about this "big, long-term marital thing," but in the space of the interview she found comedic relief and a sense of release by sharing the story of this conflict with a stranger.

   Leonda also winds up sorting through the trash left by their messy roommate, in order to sort recyclable from non-recyclable materials. Quinn describes a similar recycling dynamic in her household. She will also take items that she believes are recyclable out of the trash bin at her job at put them into the office recycling bin, though she admits that she isn't always sure of the rules and occasionally learns she is wrong. Quinn and her husband are both vegans, primarily for animal welfare reasons, though the environment is also a major consideration in their everyday choices like food and transportation. Despite shared priorities, Quinn's husband places a greater premium on comfort and convenience when it comes to getting things done.

Quinn: My husband does consider the environment for sure, but
            I think I get more anal about certain things like running
            the heat. If there is an item that as a little bit of plastic but
            is mostly paper, I'll rip off the plastic and put the paper in
            the recycling. My husband isn't as good about the recycling.
            I get pretty anal about the recycling. And sometimes he
            will take a Car2Go [short-term car rental] home. And it is
            probably because he's running late, but I would never put
            our money toward that. To me it doesn't make sense when
            there's a bus right there.

Different sustainability knowledge or priorities doesn't always lead to spousal conflict, as in the case with Rob and Rebecca.

Rob: Let's be clear—Rebecca is driving most all of these decisions.
            And I am completely OK with that. She has a passion and

an education for it, and I don't. Since our values are basically in accordance, I'm like, "Cool. Let's roll with it."

Rob appreciates Rebecca's knowledge and dedication to their sustainability practices, and their joint commitment to pragmatically balancing their pro-environmental and community-oriented priorities with what Rebecca calls her "sanity" helps them avoid disagreements over anything becoming "too extreme." Wendy told me that her wife's commitment to sustainability is inspiring and is something she loves about her, but it means that Wendy is sometimes playing catch-up with the new information guiding their household decisions. This is true even though it is Wendy and not her wife who works in the sustainability industrial complex.

But sometimes, even in households where both adults have very strong sustainability priorities and knowledge, conflict emerges over sustainability practices becoming harmful to household members. Jess enjoys running very long distances, but her refusal to replace worn-out footwear causes her physical harm.

Jim: Jess buys nothing. Almost nothing. We have to force her to buy work clothes. You buy nothing! I bought workout shoes for you because yours had no soles on them, so you couldn't *function*.

The damage that Jess' thriftiness was inflicting on her body concerns her husband, who intervenes. Jim was one of my informants who was the most attuned to reducing the environmental impact of his consumption, but this environmental concern has limits—he does not want household sustainability practices and priorities to harm the health of his family.

Differences in indoor comfort temperatures occur in households without an ecological orientation, but in my set of households the stakes are not purely about budget anxieties and comfort preferences but concern for the environmental consequences of heating and cooling choices. Several of my informants insist on keeping the winter temperature of their homes so low that their spouses are uncomfortable. Quinn, Orla, and Gloria would prefer to keep their home temperatures cooler in the winter than their husbands.

Gloria: My husband makes a lot of the heating and cooling decisions because I don't want to spend the money. I would prefer to not use the heat at all. I would prefer to put on my wool socks and some sweatshirts. We keep it low ... like 65 [degrees Fahrenheit, or 18.3 degrees Celsius]. I would want it at 60 [degrees Fahrenheit, or 15.6 degrees Celsius], and my husband would want it at 70 [degrees Fahrenheit,

or 21.1 degrees Celsius], so we settle on 65. And then I try
to supplement with the wood stove. In the spring and the
fall, it's just off. Once it's 65 outside, it's off.

Gloria would prefer to not run the heat at all, but compromises with her
husband by picking a temperature between their two preferences

Heating became a clearly gendered conflict when men controlled the
heating equipment in a way that made their wives too cold. Ivy and
Ian represent one of the more extreme cases. Their home—which is in
general disrepair—does not have central heating and has only one working
baseboard heater in their child's room. In the winter Ivy needs to lie under
blankets in the living room as soon as she gets home from work. She
describes herself as a "whiny" for not being able to adequately cope with
indoor temperatures between 50 and 60 degrees Fahrenheit (or 10 and
15.6 degrees Celsius), an indoor temperature that is potentially dangerous
to human health. Ivy is frustrated at times with their rickety old house and
wishes there were heating equipment, but Ian seems not to mind as much.

Victor is the one in his household who knows how to program the
thermostat, and he set it to 62 degrees Fahrenheit (or 16.7 degrees
Celsius) during the day when only Vanessa is usually home. This portion
of the interview was extremely uncomfortable for me as a researcher, and
represented the most forceful argument that I witnessed between any of
my informants:

Kirstin:	When it's cold outside, what temperature is comfortable for you inside?
Vanessa:	What temperature is *comfortable*, or what the furnace is set at?
Kirstin:	What temperature the furnace is set at. Is there a difference between the two of you for what temperatures you each feel comfortable at?
Vanessa:	[laughing] Yeah! The furnace is at 62? 61? [degrees Fahrenheit, or 16.7 and 16.1 degrees Celsius]
Victor:	[interrupting] No! Ok, so … If we're going to be home in the living space …
Vanessa:	[interrupting] No! That's not true!
Victor:	Then it would be like …
Vanessa:	You make me click it up!
Victor:	Well, that is your choice. If we're going to be home, it's at 66 [degrees Fahrenheit, or 18.9 degrees Celsius].
Kirstin:	Have you programmed the thermostat?
Victor:	Yes.
Kirstin:	So you're the *Thermostat Programmer?*
Victor:	[laughing] Yes.

Vanessa:	So when the kids are home from school, it bumps up to 66 or 65 [degrees Fahrenheit, or 18.9 and 18.3 degrees Celsius]..
Victor:	The daytime temperature defaults to 62 [degrees Fahrenheit, or 16.7 degrees Celsius].
Kirstin:	And in the daytime, you are at home?
Vanessa:	Yes.
Victor:	Well, she could also be at school. She volunteers at school. So if you're home, and you get chilled, then you can turn it up. Well, but if you're at school then the default is that we will keep it at 62 [degrees Fahrenheit, or 16.7 degrees Celsius] until the kids get home.
Vanessa:	And I just drink more hot tea and make sure I have a sweater.

Victor seems to imply that no one is home when Vanessa is home, and that "we're going to be at home" or "in the living space" when he and the children are at home. It is as if Vanessa's presence in the home is invisible to Victor—she is part of the furniture, literally. A nonperson whose comfort doesn't matter to Victor. For Victor, the home only needs to be heated for himself and the children. Sixty-two degrees Fahrenheit (or 16.7 degrees Celsius) is much colder than Vanessa would like. Each day she must manually increase the temperature to 66 degrees Fahrenheit (or 18.9 degrees Celsius) if she would like to feel comfortable, but generally she just remains uncomfortable or takes other steps to feel less cold. Victor will not change the thermostat program, figuring that Vanessa might have occasional obligations outside the home so it is better to have a low default setting that she can increase rather than the reverse, which could potentially be wasteful.

Some sets of spouses have different priorities in the sustainability realm. Orla is far more waste-conscious than Owen, and she would prefer to keep their home colder during the winter to save resources.

Orla:	If he doesn't feel warm enough, he is more likely to hit the button and turn the heat up. I try not to do that. I would put on a sweater or drink warm drinks.
Owen:	That is your cheapness coming out.

Orla's strong environmental priority for avoiding waste, not shared by Owen, is derided by him as "cheapness" in this tense exchange. Nicole wishes Nathan wouldn't spend his time fixing cheap things that could be replaced, and Nathan is less interested in recycling than Nicole is. Nathan uses "OCD" (obsessive compulsive disorder) as a shorthand for different focuses and priorities.

Nathan: There are varying degrees of OCD in this household. There are issues that I am OCD on and she's not, and vice versa. And the recycling is something she is OCD on and I'm not. We both do it, but she will take things out of the garbage to fix it. I won't clean out a grody can.

Nicole: We have debates all the time about fixing things that we could replace. I add the financial piece. It is just not worth the effort. Your time is a fixed commodity.

Gloria sees the differences in sustainability priorities between her spouse and herself as a benefit, since it allows the household to follow through on a larger number of sustainability practices.

Gloria: We divide the work very evenly, it's very 50–50. The strength of our interest varies, so it kind of comes out as a wash. He's very interested in not buying new stuff. He's very driven to find used stuff. He is very motivated to do that work. And sometimes I'm like, "IKEA is like, right there! They have solar panels on their roof, it's fine!" It's easier for me to fail in certain realms that he's very strong in, and vice versa.

Like many of my informants, Gloria views the division of labor in her household as egalitarian, though this may or may not be the case.

Conflicts also arose in households where only one of the spouses had interests or priorities in the sustainability realm. Mike told me very matter-of-factly, "I have no idea what my values are," and "I care about the environment, but I don't do the day to day." He did not want to participate in the interview, but Mina encouraged him to sit with us and he did join reluctantly. Mike spent the interview with his arms crossed over his chest, and occasionally rolled his eyes at my questions. Mike does not appear to *disagree* with Mina's interest in natural living and he is not hostile to environmental concerns. In fact, he is pro-environment—he loves hiking and nature, and when Trump was elected in 2016, Mike decided he wanted to give money to the Sierra Club, an environmental nonprofit, in response. However, he does not do any of the research or work involved in Mina's sustainability practices. Mina tells me, "When I start getting into GMOs and parabens and phthalates land, he tunes me out." He also prefers not to eat the vegetarian food she makes for herself and the children—he says he "loves GMOs." Mina explains that Mike's lack of interest in her natural living practices are similar to her lack of interest in technology. She trusts that Mike will research and take care of her technology needs, so she doesn't need to invest any time or effort into that area of their life. She says that she believes Mike trusts her to research their health and environmental choices (both for themselves and the children).

She thinks that if he needed to that he would show more interest and put in the effort, but he knows she has it covered. Mike has adapted to Mina's new interest by taking a nonconfrontational but slightly defensive approach, at least as far as his interactions with me went.

But again, these differences did not always lead to conflicts. Heather describes trying to be sensitive to her non-sustainability-oriented spouse and his needs:

Heather: I constantly feel like I'm changing things to be more sustainable, and I wonder how much more my husband can take and how much more of his lifestyle can be changed. He's on board, but I feel like it is at least once a week that I'm coming to him with a new idea. We can eat this, and now we can't eat this. And now we can't eat gluten. And he's just like, "I don't know what to eat. I don't know what I can feed the kids when we're out. It's really hard." And so he buys a gluten-free macaroni and cheese in a box. And I'm like, "That's why we did Whole30 [fad elimination diet]! So we don't have to buy that stuff!" But he needs the simplicity for being able to feed the kids.

Heather's husband is supportive of her sustainability efforts. However, he is responsible for food shopping and food preparation when Heather is working long nursing shifts, and sometimes gets confused about what food is OK to buy or feed to their children. Despite these concerns for her husband's ability to cope with their dietary changes, Heather is forging ahead with their whole foods-based diet.

It appears that conflict between spouses is sometimes decreased in households where one spouse has been given specific jurisdiction over sustainability-related decisions and the other spouse goes along, such as in the case of Rob and Rebecca, Heather and her spouse, and Mike and Mina. In these households, sustainability is treated as the dominion of the wives and the husbands go along with the decisions because they assume that these decisions are consistent with their shared values, in the best interests of their children, or, in the case of Mike, represent an area of household decision-making that he avoids altogether. Decision-making and research into environmental choices and practices, the subject of Chapter 7, is clearly assigned to the women in these three heterosexual relationships where the wives are the driving force behind sustainability practices and priorities in the household. However, there were even more heterosexual-couple households in my sample where it was husbands and not wives whose research and sustainability concerns were the drivers for household decision-making.

Conflicts between adults and their own parents

Conflicts over environmental priorities and practices also emerge not just within households but in close personal relationships across households. Few of my informants grew up in environmentally oriented households, so their parents frequently had different priorities than my informants, and this sometimes caused conflicts or disagreements.

Grandparents attempting to help out by purchasing toys and other items for their grandchildren cause problems for Penny and Fiona, single mothers who appreciate their parents' willingness to help but wish they would do so in a way that was consistent with sustainability priorities. Penny's parents buy poorly made plastic toys:

Penny: [My children] get presents from their grandparents, and they'll be these plastic horrible things that they tend to not even really use. So it's a balance—how pushy should I be to ask them to stop sending us that stuff, versus how much should I just let it drop?

But Penny tries to be diplomatic, and struggles with knowing when to intervene. Fiona's parents also don't buy the right things, and she has to educate them about what to buy so that their help is consistent with her priorities.

Fiona: Yeah, there have been a couple disagreements with my parents over kids' toys. I'm trying to avoid plastic-y stuff, and just more *stuff*. Like you saw, he will entertain himself for half an hour with kitchen implements. So very few toys is my goal. So family gets him more stuff than I'd like him to have. And I rotate stuff out just so that I don't have it all out at once. There have been some uncomfortable moments of wishing they would be thinking about things more the same as me. Or wishing they had more time to do research. Because my mom works full-time, too, she'll order something online. But I feel like she's gotten more consistent with asking, "What exactly do you want?" and they'll contribute more in those ways.

This is difficult for Fiona to negotiate as a single mother on a limited budget who appreciates the help from her parents, but she is sympathetic to her mother's own time constraints as a full-time worker.

Some conflicts arise not out of the grandparents' attachment to consumer culture but rather to thrift. Emily describes Eric's mother as cheap and a bargain hunter, while for Emily sustainability practices are worth the extra money, time, and effort.

Emily: I make Eric's mom use only physical barrier sunscreens on the kids, and she just rolls her eyes at me. "But the spray is so easy!" And I'm like, "You can't use the spray on the kids." I don't really argue with her about very much of anything, but that was the one thing where I was like "I have to ask you to not use the spray sunscreen. I know it's easy. I know it is." But it's just not proven to be safe.

Eric: Our parents are putting in some effort to meet us halfway. They know that we care about those things, and they will let us drive that. And we try to meet them halfway. Like we try to *bring* the sunscreen as opposed to us expecting them to change what they do, and expecting them to have certain things available to use on the children.

However, as Eric explains, he and Emily go out of their way to accommodate their parents and make it as easy as possible for them to follow their sustainability practices. Andrew and Amy similarly struggle with the thrift-mindedness of Amy's East Asian immigrant father, who has been living with them part of the time to help out with the children and other tasks.

Andrew: Amy's father is more traditional. He's been living with us a bit, sort of on and off to help with kids as we're juggling our schedules, and he is much more traditional in his food-buying practices. Much more traditional in the sense that he gets everything from WinCo [budget warehouse-style supermarket chain] and Safeway [conventional middle-of-the-road supermarket chain] and these kinds of places. And so there is a little bit of a tension there sometimes, right? In that, especially when it comes to like raw produce, things that you aren't cooking, like lettuce. There's certain things that I really would prefer were organic versus like mass farmed with whatever chemicals are being used to grow it.

Amy: Sometimes we just mention it, or we try to say, "There are certain things, if you need it, then put it on a list or tell us, and we'll go get it." But, it's an especially difficult time with our schedules, so he tries to take that burden away by going to the store and buying stuff, and it's hard and he won't really take money from us, but his biggest concern is cost.

Andrew: Yeah, he's all about cost.

Amy: So it's a difficult interplay right now.

Andrew and Amy deeply appreciate Amy's father's help during a challenging period when time is particularly scarce, and they try to be respectful of his priorities and budget. However, avoiding conventional produce is very important to their household, so they are still working out ways to accommodate this difference in priorities. Eric and Emily, however, had moved out of state to get extra childcare help from Eric's parents. This arrangement ultimately didn't work out for their household in part due to these conflicts over priorities, and they returned to Portland.

Dayna and David's parents give them a hard time about their old car, bicycle commuting, and small home. The couple like to have "less stuff," and their parents are particularly upset that the couple give away family heirlooms on Craigslist (an online classifieds site):

David: Yeah my mom definitely feels like an emotional attachment to everything that was passed down from her parents. Like their artwork and their stuff and holds on to it very dearly. And when something comes our way, we're kind of like, "Eeeeeh. Craigslist!" And she's horrified by that notion.

Dayna: Less is more. We are trying to rid ourselves of the concern that just because there is something you own that someone spent a lot of money on at some point, and now you have it … but it's like a stone around your neck. Just let it go! Get rid of it! That's definitely a difference of opinion we have between us and our parents.

For David and Dayna, these heirlooms represent the materialist values of their parents. Wendy, who grew up in South America, shared a more humorous story about her rancher parents, who told her jokingly that they had no issues when she came out as a lesbian but that they might disown her if she became a vegetarian.

But some of the interactions are more antagonistic and involve name-calling, or unhealthy, or even what may have been abusive relationships during my informants' childhoods. These conflicts are often heightened with family members who do not share the political perspective or environmental priorities of my informants. My interviews were conducted shortly after Donald Trump was inaugurated as president, at a time when political tensions in the United States were particularly high and Portland was experiencing an uptick in White supremacist activity.

Andrew's father makes fun of him for the contradictions involved in some of his choices, and Penny has a tense relationship with her father, who does not share her pro-environmental values.

Andrew: We have this woodburning stove that we use a little bit. My dad who is *super* conservative keeps like poking at us, "You know that's like the most polluting way to heat your eco-friendly house! You guys are polluting the earth!"

Penny: My dad will call me a tree hugger and a crazy eco-person.

Both Gloria and Heather have periods where they cut off communication with their mothers because conflicts over priorities and parenting get so heated.

Gloria: My mother is hardcore Republican crazy. I'm in a phase of deciding whether or not I will maintain a friendship with my mother because it's gotten quite toxic. With my mother there is so much conflict. The differences in our values are so pointed.

Heather interprets her mother's lack of sustainability priorities as indicating she doesn't care about Heather or the children.

Heather: You can speak to someone like my mom, who is a Republican, who could have voted to have the non-GMO bill [in California] passed. But she chose to vote against it because she felt like she is older now and she wasn't affected. And that made me so angry. Because what about her children, her grandchildren, her grandchildren's children, and the environment that they're going to be living in. That's a huge conflict.

She will go a couple of years at a time without talking to her mother, but ultimately caves and decides to maintain a relationship because she feels it is important for her children to know their grandmother. At the core of each of these conflicts between my informants and their parents are differing priorities and values and how those differences influence practices.

Conflicts between adults and children

Sustainability conflicts between adults and children generally revolve around teaching children the sustainability priorities and practices of the household. Vanessa tells me that her children complain that their line-dried towels are scratchy, to which she responds, "Just use it! It's clean!" and then sarcastically added, "Soooo sorry!" Several respondents discussed teaching their children to avoid wasting resources around the house. Carrie, Ivy, and Owen and Orla told me about talking to their children about conserving water.

Carrie: I remember pretty early on telling them, "Turn off the faucet, save some water for the fish." But we had explained in the past that we need to conserve water.

Ivy: Outside when she's playing with the hose. "What are you doing? You left the hose on!" So I tell her, this is why you need to do this. That's where those lessons come from, normally when she's doing something that she's not supposed to be doing!

However, Owen and Orla found that these lessons can be complicated to teach young children who don't yet have a concept of what "waste" means:

Owen: Our oldest kid is a terrible water waster. Both of us are constantly on him like, "Shut it off! Don't waste water!"

Orla: I realized the other day that I was telling him all the time not to waste water, and it occurred to me that he might not know what I meant when I was saying that. So I asked him if he knew what I meant when I told him not to waste something, and he said, "Nope!" So I had to explain! We are trying to train them and encourage them not to waste, but I think the grasp is still pretty loose.

Ian also struggles to find age-appropriate ways to communicate with his daughter about his household's sustainability practices and priorities, and the reasons behind them.

Ian: If she doesn't eat all of her food, I talk about what that means for the environment because it took a lot of energy to make that food, and then there's the off gassing. She's six and it's probably not going to stick, but I want to have those conversations with her because it's important to us.

Similarly, children struggle to turn off lights in empty rooms, something that is also related to their difficulty in understanding the concept of "waste."

Heather: See? I just turned the lights off, and my daughter was like, "Why did you just turn that light off?" In the kitchen that nobody's in!?

Amy: I've been trying to talk about leaving the lights on and things like that, and they just have no concept of wasting electricity.

Chris linked this propensity for children to waste resources to global warming with some dark humor.

Chris: I think about it a lot with the gas fireplace. They turn
           on that fireplace, and I'm just like, "You're just killing
           yourself slowly!!!" [laughing] I didn't say that to them, but
           I thought that.

Chris implied his children's use of a natural gas fireplace insert was hastening
their own deaths due to global warming. And Quinn has conversations
linking their practices to larger global humanitarian issues when her son,
who she adopted internationally from a less developed country, complains
about biking home from school in the rain:

Quinn: If my son is complaining on the bike ride home because it's
           raining, I believe he needs to learn to deal with that. And
           I tell him that there are kids who walk much further than
           this every day just to get water.

Being a child in these families means learning the priorities and practices
of the household's culture. Part of the unwaged work that takes place in
these households is socializing children into pro-environmental priorities
and unconventional ways of getting things done that may conflict with
mainstream culture.

Conflicts between children and the outside world

Several of my informants expressed that they are aware that the lifestyle
and choices they are making for their children are outside the mainstream
and may impact the way that their children interact with their peers. They
recall the pressures they experienced themselves as children and teenagers,
and don't want their children to experience negative consequences
because of the unconventional priorities and practices of their households.
Penny dislikes the plastic children acquire from places like arcades and
birthday parties, but she also understands these items are part of a typical
childhood experience.

Penny: I wish I could be more rigid and not allow any plastic into
           the house. But at the same time, I recognize that it would
           be hard to be the kid of someone who was rigid like that.

She decides not to be "rigid" because she is aware that putting these kinds of
limitations on her children could be stifling and cause them social problems
with their peers.

   Chris is strongly against consumerism as part of his environmental
priorities. He is trying to teach his children to share these values, while at

the same time trying to be understanding of the pressures his kids might be under with their peers at school.

Chris: Yeah, there were kids at school who were really into Pokémon, and now he's got a couple other friends that are into these soccer cards. So he was actually really open about it, and I said, when you buy those is it just because you want something shiny? Which I totally understand, because shiny is important. Or are you trying to impress your friends? What are your motivations? And he was like, "Well, it's a little bit of both." And I was talking to him about that more in terms of well, to me it is much more impressive when you can show your friends something that you made or something that you can do versus something that just anyone can buy. That to me isn't particularly impressive. And that's maybe not the perfect example, but I remember a different conversation where he was talking about wanting to buy some other things, and I'm not remembering what it was off the top of my head, but I remember saying to him, "When I find myself in that situation … when I just want this thing so I can have it, but it doesn't have any real bearing on my life or it's not going to last or I'm not going to be able to use it do to something with … Well, then I just feel like I should just punch myself in the face because I just want something." [laughing] So you know, maybe not the best language with an eight-year-old …

He approached the conversation with his son with humor but also sensitivity and empathy, telling his son he understands the appeal of "shiny" consumer culture and explaining why it isn't in line with his values. Just as Chris sees running the natural gas fireplace as equivalent to "killing yourself slowly" by hastening global warming, participating in consumer culture is the same as punching yourself in the face. Orla feels that her children are still too young for these types of conversations about consumerism and consumer culture, but she says she is looking forward to sharing her values with them.

Orla: I think a lot about what I want them to learn about consumerism and the impacts of the choices that they make. They're too young to understand money, but I'm looking forward to having those discussions with them. I remember having those discussions with my parents when they taught me that I don't need to buy everything that I see that I like. Maybe it's just a temporary desire and having this thing wouldn't really make my life that much better.

Gloria homeschools her children, who don't have much exposure to devices or technology.

Gloria: To a fault, my kids don't have any experience with devices, video games, apps … I think they're going to be at a disadvantage.

For now, she is happy with the way things are, but she worries that this lack of exposure to technology might be harmful in the long run, as it might disadvantage her children socially, scholastically, or even potentially professionally if they lack certain technological skills.

Amy is strict about what her children can eat, but she is flexible when it comes to school and birthday parties. In her view, being balanced is important, to avoid social problems for the children.

Amy: The kids eat school lunch on Thursdays for pizza day. I assume it's not good, but I think we also try to practice a balance. Like try not to be too crazy about things as long as it's not the norm. If there is a birthday party, they are going to have cake and whatever that cake is, but we're never going to buy stuff that has food coloring and frosting.

My informants see elements of the conventional, outside world as harmful to their children, but at the same time they want their children to grow up into healthy, well-adjusted adults. Picking how much conventional outside influence to allow is a balancing act, and each household strikes their own balance that depends on their unique priorities, resources, and constraints, but also on the developmental stages of their children.

Internal conflicts and guilt

My informants care deeply about sustainability and believe that their everyday choices have important impacts. This means that when they make a choice that isn't aligned with their priorities they sometimes feel guilt and remorse. Carrie likes to travel and finds that difficult to reconcile with her knowledge that the carbon impacts of travel are much larger than many of the everyday carbon impacts she works to avoid. Because Eric and Emily both work full-time, the household relies on purchases from Amazon.com frequently for the convenience and time saving of having items delivered to their home.

Emily: I always feel a little guilty when I get something from Amazon or something that is egregiously packaged.

She knows this decision is not good for the environment, and feels bad about this compromise in her values for convenience's sake.

Carrie:	I have to be way better about all of the packaging, and I've taken to ordering things online, and then I feel bad about packaging.
Kirstin:	What drives the decision to order things online?
Carrie:	Ease and time constraints.

Guilt over Amazon.com purchases and the associated packaging was a fairly common subject that informants brought up. They feel that packaging is bad for the environment, but they also feel such pressing time constraints that the ease of ordering needed items online is worth the emotional discomfort of dealing with the packaging once the items arrive.

Heather also found it necessary to stop cloth diapering after she had her third child.

Heather:	It [cloth diapers] was a priority, but when it became too much work, I had to let something go. And I still have a little bit of guilt about not doing it as long as I could have.

Penny compares herself to other people she knows who consider themselves sustainable, but don't appear to have the same kind of guilt that she does about driving places to save time.

Penny:	I drive a lot, but I feel a lot of guilt about that. A lot of my friends will drive everywhere, and it would *never* occur to them to take the bus. I find myself driving a lot more than I ever thought I would. I relinquished that and feel bad about that.

She knows that she is doing better than most of her peers, but her awareness of environmental issues means she also knows she could be doing more.

Conclusion

My informants are challenged by the differences in mundane practices and their social meanings in their close personal relationships. These conflicts can be heightened because of their deliberate attempts to carry out mundane everyday tasks in ways that differ from the "mainstream" and the high stakes involved in their motivations for making these interventions in mundane practices—the continued well-being of their families and the planet. Most of the reports of conflicts by my informants seem to involve the sort of back-and-forth compromise that one might expect any time human beings come together to work out differences in daily life, even when comments sounded hostile, such as Owen calling out his wife's "cheapness." However, some conflicts involved such intensity that they brought relationships into crisis due to divergences in values and priorities, such as in the relationships between Heather, Penny, and Gloria, and their own parents. By far the most disturbing interaction I witnessed in the entire course of this research was the account of Victor's controlling and dismissive behavior toward his wife and their disagreements over thermostat temperatures, as Victor seemed to treat his wife as a nonperson in their household. And I was frequently touched by the expressions of guilt and frustration from my informants as they experienced internal conflict and struggled to balance their sustainability priorities with their busy lives as parents of young children in contemporary capitalism. Chapter 9 will delve further into these struggles to balance seemingly impossible choices and the trade-offs involved.

9

"How Do We Live with Ourselves?"

Overview

Possibly the most central idea in neoclassical economics can be summed up in a single line from Kevin Costner's 1995 flop of a post-apocalyptic film about life after the melting of the polar ice caps: "Nothing's free in Waterworld." Or from a popular introductory economics textbook, describing the concept of opportunity costs: "To get one thing that we like, we usually have to give up another thing that we like. Making decisions requires trading off one goal against another" (Mankiw 2012, 4). Trade-offs may be what neoclassical economics is all about, but this hinges on a concept of scarcity, popularized in anglophone economics by Lionel Robbins (2007 [1932], 15), so trade-offs must be understood in context. The economy, society, and cultures in which we live influence decisions that neoclassical economists often model as made freely by identical autonomous individuals. Rather, the organization of capitalist society compels some activities and constrains others.

In Chapter 2 of this book, I discussed my Marxist-feminist model of household production in which households, capitalist firms, and the state are linked to one another via their production processes. According to this model, households can get things done in everyday life using varying proportions of inputs—commodities purchased with money from waged work, goods and services from the state, and time in the form of unwaged work—but in doing so are complicit in the reproduction of capitalist society. In Chapters 3 and 4, I described the ways my informants get things done in everyday life via mundane practices, prioritizing the things that are important to them, making use of the resources available to them, and subject to the factors that constrain them. The sustainability priorities of my informants include community well-being, the health of individual family members, nature, technology, and waste avoidance. Their resources include money, time, and know-how. My informants feel constrained in their choices by social and cultural norms, as well as a lack of accurate information about sustainability practices. This combination of priorities, resources, and constraints were different in every household. However, one striking universal complaint across all of my interviews was about a lack of time, as pro-environmental practices tend to take more time than money. These constraints frequently mean that my informants can't do everything they'd like when it comes to their sustainability values—they have to pick between a limited set of alternatives, and sometimes the compromise involved in those choices is heart-wrenching and painful.

For example, Emily had more time and energy to make the environment and sustainability a top priority prior to becoming a parent.

Emily: The realities of life are what they are, and everybody just needs to do the best they can. And just because I really am an anxious person, I really needed to be like "I can't have this on my shoulders." This can't be all up to me. I'm just going to do the best that I can, and … So in many regards, I think I've sort of stepped back from having it [environmental causes] be a driving force.

Now, with all the other responsibilities and concerns she is juggling, she feels like she is no longer able to take on the additional burden of worrying about the environment as much as she used to. She is doing her best, but her own well-being and the well-being of her family were incompatible with fully dedicating herself to environmental issues. Something had to give.

Returning to the model presented in Chapter 2, households must reproduce themselves to perpetuate their own existence day to day and intergenerationally, and in doing so contribute to the reproduction of capitalist society as a whole. The reproduction of capitalist society depends on the capitalist continually reproducing himself as a capitalist, and the worker continually reproducing herself as a worker—compelled to do so both "physically and socially" (Clarke 1995, 19–20) as they are each at once produced by the capitalist production process and reproduced by it. My model of household production shows how a variety of inputs serve as both substitutes and complements in the household production process and can be used in varying proportions. The interdependencies between the state, capitalist firms, and households—through which the continued existence of one ensures the continued existence of the others and, with this, the continued existence of capitalist society—mean that shifts in the proportions of inputs are not sufficient to change the underlying production processes that together constitute and reproduce capitalist society. Households can substitute time for money and money for time to produce goods and services for household members that are consistent with their pro-environmental values, but these changes merely alter the intensity with which the household uses one input or another (Collins 1990, 17). These substitutions fall short of what is needed to transform society—but what happens when people try to live, in Kyle's words, a "less eco-hostile" existence? Because their choices were already constrained before the choosing begins, they frequently find themselves in impossible situations.

Trade-offs between priorities are most apparent in my informants' everyday lives when it comes to budgeting their scarce time and financial resources. Some sustainability tasks they are unable to do because of not enough time or money, while some informants told me that they substitute money for time or time for money when it comes to sustainability practices. Mental and emotional energy is also in limited supply and my informants need to rest between all of their waged and unwaged work. So even when they feel like they have enough time or money, they have decided to stop or decrease their adherence to certain practices to preserve their own "sanity". A particularly poignant example of trade-offs and compromise in the lives of some of my nature-focused informants is the decision to have children despite a firmly held conviction that having children is the worst thing they could do for the environment. Balancing regular life with sustainability priorities means that my informants are frequently faced with difficult decisions, and the compromises involved make them feel guilty and upset about their inability to live in a way that is fully compatible with their ideals.

Budgeting

My informants balance their time and money to get things done in everyday life, but they do not have either in limitless supply. Sometimes, financial budgets took priority over sustainability goals. Picking organic versus conventional food is one area where the environmental impact is weighed against the costs.

Penny: I buy most produce organic, but there is give and take with certain items with the organic is much more expensive.

Jim and Wendy told me about needing to buy clothing for their children at big box mass retailers like Target, where they know the clothes were not produced sustainably or according to their values surrounding the treatment of workers.

Jim: It is depressing when we have to go to Target and get environmentally bad crappy new clothes for our kid. I guess the other option would be to get organic cotton at boutiques, but that's not really economically reasonable.

The alternative to a high-cost organic children's clothing boutique would be trying to find items in a secondhand store or free, but I was told by many parents that children's clothing is difficult to find for many age groups because the clothes get worn out and destroyed so quickly.

For other households, a lack of time caused them to abandon certain sustainability practices.

Fiona: There have been, in my life situations, where I know that I could do this [sustainability practice] but it would be TEN TIMES HARDER. So there is a little bit of selectiveness in that some things are easier than others.

Andrew: I feel like for me it's a balancing act. I have all of these things that I'm dealing with on a daily basis, with kids, and job, and whatever. I have really limited bandwidth at this point in my life, and I feel like time is becoming more and more valuable. I feel like I don't have enough of it. And so it becomes this balancing act of: what are the things that I can do, lifestyle-wise, environmentally, that are going to have the biggest impact but are not going to take insane amounts of time and energy to make happen.

Yvonne: There have been times when I was really pressed for time, and I've had to learn how to manage it better. I have three kids, and we were doing full homesteading, so we had chickens and lots of animals and I had to spend so much time caring for all of the animals, and then my children, and then the cooking, and then the cleaning on the inside as well as on the outside of the house. Now we are down to just two dogs.

Fiona tends to select the practices that are the easiest and take the least amount of time, while Andrew told me that he does a mental cost-benefit analysis to select the practices that have the highest environmental impact for the least effort. Yvonne had to give up raising livestock to be able to manage all of her competing responsibilities—regular household duties, parenting her three children, running an urban homestead, and contributing work to her husband's small permaculture business.

Several households told me about the ways they substitute time spent in unwaged work for money in getting their sustainability practices done. Yvonne quit her two jobs in the food service industry so that she could focus on intensive urban homesteading tasks like making her own laundry soap, growing much of their own produce, and making meals for her family from scratch. Yvonne's unwaged sustainability work in her household allows her family to live on one income, though she does spend about 15 hours per week working for her husband's small business. Victor sees his household's decision to substitute Vanessa's unwaged time for market purchases in larger terms.

Victor: This is the big Faustian bargain of the modern economy. People see themselves struggling to get by and cannot imagine what a 30–50 percent drop in income would do to their finances. But that's the lie. Income may drop 30–50 percent, but expenses drop an entirely commensurate amount with virtually no economic sacrifice to the family's standard of living. Thirty to fifty hours a week, depending on full- or part-time and the amount of commuting required, is freed up to "work" for the family. Frankly, I think families with both parents working are nuts, and accounts for the falling, sub-replacement birthrates among Western countries.

Victor sees his wife's unwaged work for the family as more than replacing her lost income, and believes that it is better for families in general if women avoid working outside the home. The extra money that waged work could add to the household budget is not worth the cost. Mina is a stay-at-home mother, and while her sustainability practices are not quite as time-intensive as those of Yvonne and Vanessa, she thinks about her unwaged work in monetary terms.

Mina: I'm a stay-at-home mom and my time is my value to the household.

While few of the households I spoke with were making the same kinds of choices as Yvonne and Victor and Vanessa, most of my informants were aware that these choices were a possibility.

Rebecca: I think that the way *we* try to make sustainability choices is more expensive, but I don't think that's true in general. My brother and sister-in-law have two kids, and they grow all of their own food, they reuse a lot of things, they make their own yogurt, they do a lot of sewing, and his business is around using salvaged wood. They do it very cheaply because they have a stay-at-home parent and more of a homestead thing. They are substituting time for money.

Rebecca likes her job and working outside the home, and she doesn't particularly enjoy gardening, intensive food preparation, and crafts, so she is happy with the decision that she and Rob have made to both work for wages.

Several of the higher-income households I spoke with told me that they were aware of cheaper ways to get things done sustainably, but that because of their work schedules they wind up substituting money for unwaged time in their sustainability practices.

Owen: I feel like our more traditional career-focused jobs make it more difficult to not spend more money to be eco-conscious. Orla and I both work more than 40 hours a week, we are continually at the office, or taking care of the kids, or putting in extra hours from home. So if we want to make eco-conscious things happen, we pay to make them happen by buying certain things.

Rob: Relatively speaking, we are doing phenomenally well economically. And that gives us the privilege to make a lot of these choices with limited hassle. That makes it easier for us to make these choices.

Rob and Owen see the money that household members earn from their waged jobs as allowing them to make sustainability-oriented choices with limited difficulty, substituting money for time.

Carbon budgeting and compromise

Many of my informants think about their practices and choices in terms of their relative carbon impacts—they maintain not only a financial budget, but also a carbon budget. Having done the research necessary to gain awareness of the carbon impacts of their practices allows them to prioritize certain carbon-intensive activities over others.

Jess: I've learned about the carbon impact of beef, and it's just giant. That is just a fact that you can learn, and then you can make decisions based on that. It doesn't mean that you can't eat beef ever, but if you only eat it once a month that is a lot better than eating it once a week or every meal.

They take a pragmatic rather than perfectionist approach to making decisions to reduce carbon impact—cutting out what you can such as vacation travel or frequent beef eating.

Jim: We try to limit our airline travel, but Jess' family lives in the Midwest and I have a grandfather who lives in Southern California who is too old to travel. We've made the decision to compromise. We've made the choice not to use airline travel for vacations. But we do go to those two places by plane to see family.

Seeing family who are not within easy driving distance is something worth compromising strongly held environmental values while eliminating all other airline travel. Penny buys close to nothing new, and as an environmental educator is very aware of her environmental impacts, but she feels like seeing family is a necessity that justifies the negative environmental consequences of her choice.

Penny: I feel bad about flying, but my family all lives far away. I know a lot of people who push for taking more local trips to use less resources, and I feel like I still have to go see my family, and they live across the United States.

My eco-conscious informants know that the rest of their pro-environmental activities are just a drop in the bucket in terms of carbon impacts compared with long-distance flights.

Carrie: I feel guilty about flying in airplanes. My carbon footprint is terrible! Chris spent a brief period of time working for [climate change nonprofit], where it was all about carbon footprints. And learning about what are the worst culprits. And well, all the little things we do that are good don't nearly add up to impact of the flying places. But I really like to travel! So I am not really sure what to do about that one. Buy some carbon credits? [laughs]

Carrie laughs when she somewhat sarcastically suggests buying carbon credits to offset her plane travel—she thinks this suggestion is ridiculous and does not believe carbon credits are truly effective. Thus, there is guilt involved in making these compromises because my informants are well informed when it comes to the carbon impacts of their choices. However, my informants don't feel so guilty that they've decided to eliminate airplane travel altogether. They have limits to how far they are willing or able to go for the environment.

Giving things up for sanity

Some of my informants feel that they have enough time and money but find that they need to prioritize their mental health over certain sustainability goals. Because mental and emotional energy also need to be budgeted, many households tell me that they have been "giving things up for sanity." Penny's children are picky eaters, and she will buy foods like processed meats to ensure the children are getting enough protein and to simplify her own life.

Penny: My kids love to eat meat. Like gross meat that I don't like. Packaged meat that I would never eat. I would normally say we don't need to buy this much meat, but it is easy to put that in their lunch and they'll actually eat it, and they are getting protein. So there is a lot of give and take for me … Trying to get two kids out the door at 6:30 in the morning … I don't care! Just eat some food!

Jim is extremely conscious of the carbon impact of his choices, but he has found that strictly limiting his food purchases to minimize his environmental impact was no longer practical once he had a child.

Jim: He's a picky two-year-old. His health trumps environmental choices. If he doesn't eat, he's grumpy. So really his health and our sanity is driving some purchases of packaged food and out-of-season produce.

So that they can remain "sane", making sure that their child eats and sleeps is now a top priority for Jim and Jess. This causes them to buy food they wouldn't buy otherwise, and to run an electric heater in their child's bedroom, which they believe is bad for the environment.

The idea of prioritizing sanity was often framed as a way that my informants give themselves permission to make a less labor-intensive but also less sustainable choice.

Penny: There are times when I am cleaning out the refrigerator and I'll find a gross yogurt container or something, and I don't want to go through the pain to clean it out to recycle it. There are moments for my own sanity when I have to say, "OK in this moment, I need to just not care."
Penny: I don't want to spend my whole like revolving around not using plastic, so I have to draw a line.
Fiona: We use cloth diapers probably 90 percent of the time. Occasionally I'll get really tired of laundry or behind on the laundry, and so I'll use disposable sometimes in those situations. I have the disposables around for my own laziness … but maybe it's really just self-care. Keeping my sanity about the laundry.
Heather: We used cloth diapers for the most part with my first, and then for less time with my second, and the third she may

	have gotten maybe the first six weeks. It was a priority, but when it became too much work, I had to let something go.
Yvonne:	Occasionally when I'm feeling overwhelmed, I will buy store-bought laundry detergent instead of making it myself. Sometimes I'll buy a frozen pizza instead of making it fully from scratch to make things a little easier for myself in the day.

They recognize that it is not possible to live a perfectly sustainable life and sometimes it is necessary to allow themselves to revert to more conventional ways of getting things done, even if they find it personally upsetting to abandon certain sustainability practices in favor of their mental health and personal well-being.

Gloria takes a pragmatic approach to "sanity" out of necessity—she was unable to balance her sustainability priorities with her desire for a clean home while simultaneously caring for three young children.

Gloria:	Baby number three was born 13 months after the twins. And she was a real catalyst for letting go. It helped me learn to stop being so crazy about cleaning. But that's when things came into my life like a Swiffer [combination sweeper-mop designed to be used with disposable sweeper pads]. But I hate throwing things away, so I made a little sock thing for the Swiffer. I tried to find things that were convenient that I could adapt to my values.

To stay "sane" she found ways to compromise a little bit in each area—cleanliness and sustainability—so that she could manage the demands of her work as a mother of three young children.

While both Eric and Emily care deeply about the environment and the health of their children, Emily's personality means that she can have trouble letting go of things that are important to her. Eric is more laid-back, and has encouraged Emily make herself and her own well-being a priority too.

Eric:	I think it's largely a bandwidth issue. We both work and we have two kids under ten. Day-to-day survival starts to take more of a priority. Some of those [environmental] micro decisions start to fall off a little bit.
Emily:	We're seven and a half years into this parenting game now, and I think there was a point where our son was two, and he was a really challenging toddler, that I think it was like "something has to give." I was really stressed out. Eric doesn't really get stressed out, but he was not happy with me being

unhappy. There comes a point where you have to be like, "I can't do it all."

A similar pattern emerged in my conversation with Rob and Rebecca. Rebecca has a strong community-minded approach to her sustainability priorities, but she also values her own well-being—what she and Rob called "sanity" several times during our conversation. It was clear that she and Rob have an ongoing dialogue about balance between time-intensive sustainability practices and their ability to take care of personal needs and the needs of their young children.

Rebecca: I feel like in general, and it's because capitalism does this, people prioritize themselves over everyone together. Which I do, which *we* do, when we decide *not* to do certain [sustainability] things so we can maintain our sanity. But it makes it hard to have respect for people who prioritize themselves all the time.

Rob: We are trying to reduce our impact on the environment, but we are very cool with making compromises for what's within our sanity and financial resources.

In another part of our interview, Rebecca brought up the concept of "sanity" again.

Rebecca: There is not really time during the weekend between grocery shopping and kids' activities to make a special trip to the recycling center, but down the line I can see that those are things that we would want to do. Right now, we are prioritizing sanity.

Likewise, Mina told me about the limits to her sustainability practices, and trying to find a balance that works for her.

Mina: I hate buying out-of-season fruit. I guess I could have been canning all summer, but that is just not a reasonable expectation for my life.

While she finds it upsetting to buy fruit out of season, preserving local in-season produce doesn't fit with her lifestyle and priorities. My informants find it necessary to give themselves permission to occasionally de-emphasize their sustainability practices, giving up some of these practices so that they can remain "sane". Rebecca doesn't like to give up these sustainability practices, and she feels that doing so is in conflict with her values, but she has a limited supply of energy and feels like she has no other choice.

165

Anti-natalist informants

My informants called their children things like "water wasters," "energy hogs," or "little consumer machines" and told me that most sustainability practices don't come naturally to children. Others look forward to their children getting older, when they believe they will have more time to get back to some of the more time-intensive sustainability practices or environmental activism that they had abandoned when they became parents. For some of my informants, the decision to have children at all represents the ultimate compromise of their sustainability priorities. They told me they believe having biological children is one of the worst things a person can do for the environment.

Quinn: There is a car-free family here who has five biological children. And maybe they'll all end up car-free when they grow up, or maybe three of them will end up with cars one day. And maybe she'll end up with 25 grandkids. There's no guarantee that the children will have the same values. In fact, maybe they'll grow up to be really opposed to those environmental values. So now that I think about it, I don't think they are more sustainable than me because I don't have biological children.

Chris believes the decision he and Carrie made to become parents to two children was a major concession of his environmental values. Like several others in the study, it is Chris' view that being a parent is antithetical to sustainability, but it was a compromise he made for his wife, who wanted children.

Chris: I think raising kids in a First-World country is probably the least sustainable thing that we can do! But you know, you make your choices in relationships.

Kyle and Kelly decided to have only one child for environmental reasons, citing the reasoning in *Maybe One: A Case for Smaller Families*, McKibben's 1999 polemic on the environmental destruction associated with the lifestyles of people living in the United States.

Kyle: We live in one of the richest countries in the world, most highly consumptive. And we decided to have a child! And that is one of the worst, most consumptive things to do is to create another person who in turn is going to consume more.

Kelly: We got together knowing we wanted to have a family. But
          we have decided to only have one child, partly because of
          our environmental values, and also [laughing] because it's a
          lot of fucking work!

Kyle and Kelly entered their relationship knowing that they wanted to be
parents, and they saw having just one child as an appropriate compromise
of their environmental values. That being said, they do not shy away from
their conviction that this decision was bad for the environment. Jim and
Jess also emphasize that they have retained their view that having children
is bad for the environment even after becoming parents.

Jim: We still feel that having a kid is a bad environmental choice.
          It's not that we've changed our mind about the environmental
          impact of a kid. We just changed our mind and decided we
          were willing to compromise or forgo our ethics. We decided
          it was more important to have a kid than to sustain that
          environmental ethic.

They entered their relationship agreeing that they did not want to have
biological children on environmental grounds. Later in their relationship, Jim
and Jess decided they wanted to be parents and tried to adopt, but became
frustrated by their inability to find adoption resources and support for couples
who were adopting for environmental reasons. Eventually, they decided
that their desire to be parents was more important than their environmental
values and that they needed to make a compromise.

Jim: Some people think they are environmentally minded, but in
          my mind the worst environmental choice you can make is to
          have a family, to have kids. That speaks to me to enormous
          hypocrisy to say you're an environmentalist and to have kids.
          But it is such a sensitive subject because it is a very personal
          decision for people.

They still struggle with guilt over their decision to have a biological child,
though they do not regret becoming parents. However, they agreed that
two children would feel like too much of a compromise of their priorities.

Jess: It is hard, you don't want other people to feel judged. So
          many people we know are having second kids. Having one
          kid seems like a compromise of sorts. If I had a second kid,
          I would feel like I'd just given up on all of my values.

Jim and Jess see their environmentalist friends who had more than one child as hypocritical. Quinn always knew that she did not want to have biological children on environmental and humanitarian grounds.

Quinn: I've never had a desire to have a biological child for environmental and humanitarian reasons. It doesn't make sense to bring another child into this world. There are kids who don't have homes or families.

Her husband *did* want biological children, but he went along with her plan for an international adoption, saving the money by prioritizing the adoption and having a simple wedding and no honeymoon trip.

Quinn: We knew going into adopting that it was going to be expensive, and so we decided to have a pretty minimal wedding. It cost us $400 altogether. We didn't have a honeymoon, because we knew we would be traveling as part of the adoption. But we have friends who have told us that adoption is too expensive, but spent money on an expensive Prius or an expensive wedding and honeymoon. But it's just a matter of priorities. If you want the adoption, you can make it happen.

Chris and Kyle believe that it is specifically raising children in the United States, an advanced industrialized country, which is bad for the environment. In their view, the environmental damage associated with having children in a less developed country would be lower. Quinn declined to have biological children on environmental grounds, and instead moved a child from a less developed country to Portland, Oregon, where he is likely to consume exponentially more resources over the course of his life. She and her family make regular long-distance plane trips to visit her son's birth family, since Quinn and her husband felt it was important for their son to know his biological family and their culture. It can often feel as if there are no easy answers for these ecologically conscious adults who are trying to balance their pro-environmental values with other wants and needs.

Conclusion

The conventional introductory economics course teaches students that "making decisions requires trading off one goal against another" (Mankiw 2012, 4). This is exactly what my informants are doing when, as I've described in this chapter, they compromise their environmental values for other wants and needs, or substitute time and money for one another to get things done in everyday life in a way that feels consistent with their environmental priorities. But they are frequently dissatisfied with the outcome and frustrated by the compromises they feel forced to make.

My informants frequently agonize over even the smallest decisions and feel guilty about not making the right sustainability choices. Even the households who were making some of the most extreme interventions in conventional practices expressed the view that they weren't doing enough.

Chris: I almost didn't respond [to the request for participants] because I didn't feel like what we are doing is anywhere close to being sustainable, even though we're relatively … compared to other people, we're probably farther along. I studied environmental science in college. And honestly, a lot of choices and things that we do are not sustainable in terms of the long-term carrying capacity of the planet. Including having two kids, food choices, and garbage creation and the breadth of choices that we make throughout our lives. Like living in a detached, large single-family house. Even though it's relatively energy-efficient, we're not net zero and we are generating garbage.

Kyle: When I saw the flyer for this study about sustainable families, the first thing I thought was that I don't think we are sustainable. I don't think that what we are doing is sustainable. Maybe less eco-hostile. I don't think the life I live is eco-friendly. It is just by degrees less eco-hostile. I do want to live, and I do want to have a child. We aren't ready to move to a developing country. So the question is, "How do we live with ourselves?"

At the end of the day, there appears to be no right answer and no perfectly sustainable household with young children—just a lot of people trying to do the best they can to bring their everyday lives into alignment with their values despite many factors working against them.

Heather: My husband tells me that I can't do it all, and I understand that, but we can make little steps and those will all be helpful. Anything we can make ourselves helps us get away from consumerism and capitalism. Companies aren't ethical. They don't have our health and best interests in mind. They're motivated by their own personal wealth and gain.

My informants are part of capitalist society and contribute to its continued existence, but at the same time are dominated by it. They are just parents who are trying to make the right choices for their families and the environment in a society that feels out of step with their sustainability priorities, but this is a heavy burden.

References

Clarke, Simon (1995) "Marx and the Market," [online], Available: https://homepages.warwick.ac.uk/~syrbe/pubs/LAMARKW.pdf [Accessed August 30, 2022].

Collins, Jane L. (1990) "Unwaged labor in comparative perspective: Recent theories and unanswered questions," in Jane L. Collins and Martha Giménez (eds) *Work without Wages: Comparative Studies of Domestic Labor and Self-Employment*, Albany: State University of New York Press, pp 3–24.

Mankiw, N. Gregory (2012) *Essentials of Economics* (6th edn), Mason, OH: Cengage Learning.

McKibben, Bill (1999) *Maybe One: A Case for Smaller Families*, New York: Penguin Publishing Group.

Robbins, Lionel (2007) *An Essay on the Nature and Significance of Economic Science*, Auburn, AL: Mises Institute.

10

Conclusion: "We Have Met the Enemy and He Is Us"

Over the course of this project, childhood memories of the 1992 animated film *FernGully: The Last Rainforest* kept popping into my head. In this movie, a young fairy apprentice uses the magic of the "web of life" to save the Australian rainforest from an evil anthropomorphic oil spill bent on destruction. I remember so clearly being nine years old and deeply frustrated with powerful grown-ups' inability or unwillingness to tackle the environmental devastation that weighed so heavily on my mind. I wasn't clear on what was causing the destruction of the planet—greed, ignorance, big corporations, and an evil anthropomorphic oil spill probably all seemed like plausible explanations. I could eat Rainforest Crisp cereal, put milk jugs filled with rocks in our toilet tanks, and write letters to the president, but at the end of the day I felt totally powerless and deeply angry. Adults were always telling *me* to "do the right thing"—so why were they allowing the planet to be destroyed? I felt like the flying fox and vivisection victim Batty, attempting to warn others about impending dangers and just getting ignored. I wished I had magical powers like FernGully's fairy Crysta so I, too, could save the earth.

My informants also grew up in the era of corporate oil spills, chemical disasters, acid rain, ozone depletion, deforestation, and, somewhat paradoxically, an increasing sense of *personal* responsibility for the natural environment. The iconic 1970 Earth Day poster by Walt Kelly featuring a cartoon opossum Pogo surrounded by trash broadcasts a stark message: "We Have Met the Enemy and He Is Us." My informants learned about recycling and litter in primary school from a guy dressed up in a trash heap costume, they diligently cut up their plastic six-pack rings to save wildlife, and they were bombarded with messages from promotional campaigns like Iron Eyes Cody's famous plea as he paddles his canoe through factory effluent and a discarded fast-food meal is hurled at his feet out of a moving vehicle: "People Start Pollution. People Can Stop It."

While the "Crying Indian" ad is one of the most successful U.S. public service announcements of all time (Andersen 2013, 404), less well known is the background story of this ad campaign. It was produced by a front group for the lobbying interests of disposable beverage bottling companies seeking to avoid legislation, motivated by public concerns about waste and littering, which threatened to mandate refillable glass beverage bottles and bottle deposits (Andersen 2013, 407; Strand 2008). By convincing consumers to take on the work of container disposal, beverage bottling companies were able to avoid regulation, secure their profits, and ensure that reusable individual-serving beverage packaging all but disappeared as a method for transporting liquids to their end users. This campaign and others like it that promote recycling and "doing your part" for the environment have been so successful at shifting the responsibility for the environment to households and consumers that my informant Orla now describes the experience of not being able to recycle something as *painful*.

The shift of responsibility for environmental risks from the state and corporations onto households is part of a larger pattern in late 20th- and early 21st-century United States described by Hacker (2006). As Hacker (2006) outlines, the New Deal era saw the role of the government expanded to include providing a minimum standard of living and mitigating the risk of poverty for citizens, with a particular focus on poverty in old age and childhood, due to the death of a working spouse or disability, and due to unemployment or underemployment. To attract workers, the role of employers expanded in the United States to include the provision of pensions and health insurance benefits. Over the course of the last forty years, these policies and benefits provided by the state and employers that reduced the risk to individuals of fluctuations in their wealth and health have eroded. At the same time, public awareness of environmental risks has increased, and the responsibility for dealing with these risks has likewise fallen onto households and individuals.

Producing sustainability in households

It is against the backdrop of this social history and more recent public concerns about global warming and the health impacts of chemicals that my highly ecologically conscious informants are raising young children in one of the most "sustainable" cities in the United States. In this book, I described what happens when sustainability-oriented households decide to make interventions in mundane and easy-to-overlook aspects of everyday life to bring the way they get things done into alignment with their values and priorities. Because their ability to do so is constrained by the culture, society, and economic system in which they live, there are consequences and trade-offs involved in these household-level sustainability practices. Before

172

promoting unwaged sustainability work at the household level as a solution to environmental and other problems, we must understand the full extent of these trade-offs.

The households I spoke with over the course of this research get everyday things done just like everyone else: prioritizing the things that are the most important to them, making use of the resources available to them, and constrained by the factors that limit their options. While I had expected to find relatively affluent households representing varying shades of "green" along a pro-environmental spectrum, what I discovered instead was a diverse set of informants with a set of overlapping priorities in the sustainability realm—personal health, the preservation of nature, the avoidance of waste, technology as a solution to problems, and community well-being. Two or three of these areas tended to be most important to each informant, with priorities differing between couples fairly regularly. Households also differed in the extent to which their interest in sustainability was primarily focused on protecting the members of their household or on protecting elements outside the household.

Throughout this book, I have pointed to the complicity of household production in the reproduction of capitalist society. The unwaged work component of household production is not virtuous, ennobling, or receiving inadequate credit or compensation. Rather, the model I presented in Chapter 2 points to the necessary role that household production plays in the persistence of capitalist society and the necessary interdependencies between the production that takes place in households, firms, and the state in capitalism. This unwaged work of household production represents a means of reproducing a social reality that inhibits the further development of all of those people alive today and that threatens the very existence of the planet and future generations. This unwaged work is also one input into a household production process that includes other inputs that may serve as substitutes—substitutions that alter the intensity with which the household uses one input or another (Collins 1990, 17) but that do not change the underlying household production process.

Put another way: To get things done, my informants made use of the various resources available to them. Money can be saved through additional expenditures of unwaged time and households with little time can achieve their sustainability goals by spending more money. But these resources include more than unwaged work of immediate family members and market goods and services purchased with money from waged work—my informants also receive assistance from extended family and friends and the government and nonprofits to help them get things done. Unwaged time is also used to research and gain competence in sustainability practices and is an important input into provisioning through gleaning, borrowing, and theft. These resources are employed in varying combinations and are both substitutes and complements for getting things done in everyday life in a way that feels compatible with my informants' values.

I focused the discussion here on three aspects of everyday life that have received limited scholarly attention: household waste, cleanliness, and comfort. My informants told me that the processing and removing of items that are undesirable or no longer needed from the household represent an important expression of their sustainability priorities, and that dealing with product packaging is a major source of frustration. While avoiding consumption in the first place is a priority for some households, dealing with unwanted materials through recycling, composting, resale, and giving things away for free is acceptable for others. Many of the households I spoke with decided to devote large amounts of time to cloth diapering their young children, believing this to be the most environmentally friendly choice, though as my informants Jim and Rebecca pointed out, this is likely not the case, even when the diapers are line-dried. Lacking perfect information about the efficacy of their choices, my informants are doing the best they can to do the right thing for their children, communities, and environment.

My focus on production and practices helps to reveal some of the negative consequences of placing the responsibility for environmental protection on households. Ecologically conscious households devote substantial time and money to these sustainability efforts, but their efforts frequently stimulate conflicts and the end results are rarely perfect. Constrained resources and limited information mean household members must make trade-offs between competing priorities, often under duress. Finally, the practices of my informants frequently seek to address and undo problems created at other sites and scales, such as the production, packaging, and distribution of goods. The conclusion I draw from the available evidence is that promoting household-level sustainability efforts may be misguided, as this transfer of institutional responsibility for environmental protection into households results in even greater burdens on households, whose time, money, and emotional capacities are already stretched to their limits.

Beyond depleting people physically, financially, and emotionally, many of these pro-environmental activities are ineffective at best and are self-contradictory at worse (Munro 2022). "The humanizing effort presupposes as eternal those same inhuman conditions that provoke the humanizing effort in the first place" (Bonefeld 2008, 70); I argue in Chapter 2 that these paradoxical pro-environmental activities inadvertently reproduce capitalist society, and in doing so enable the environmental devastation that motivates these practices in the first place.

Cleanliness and comfort represent areas of everyday life where meaningful changes in the household demand for resources require accompanying changes in cultural meanings and social norms. Changing thermostat settings or avoiding the use of heating and cooling appliances as a solution to indoor comfort saves money and energy but requires changing what it means to be comfortable inside and norms surrounding the sorts of actions that are appropriate to feel comfortable in hot and cold weather. While my informants generally believe that cleaning their homes with nontoxic cleansers and line-drying their laundry takes more time, other ways that they have changed everyday practices take less time—showering less often and wearing clothes more times between washings. Installing an energy-efficient clothes washing machine saves some electricity, but doesn't change underlying expectations about how often clothes should be washed, what clean towels should feel like, or who should be doing this washing and on what scale. Similarly, energy-efficient furnaces and air conditioners can be installed, but they don't change underlying expectations about what sorts of spaces people should be living in and with whom, how people should feel indoors, and the steps they should take to make it feel that way. In the same way, progressive policies such as paid family leave reinforce the expectation that the young and the sick should be cared for in households by related adults.

Ultimately, it is these underlying expectations that motivate the household demand for resources like water, electricity, natural gas, and time spent in unwaged household work. These hidden and taken-for-granted expectations—including the expectation that related people should live together in households and that this is the appropriate site and scale for raising children—become recursively embedded in our practices, appliances, infrastructures, and homes. The washing machine hookup in the basement suggests to the inhabitants that there ought to be a washing machine there. The presence of central cooling suggests that using this appliance is an appropriate way to remain comfortable during hot weather. The stock of three- and four-bedroom houses suggests that households of related people ought to live in them. Each layer reinforces the normalcy of the others and limits the possibilities for radical changes in demand and ways of getting things done.

My informants are embedded in a culture, in a society, and in a particular economic system that constrain their possible actions and choices. In everyday life, these constraints appear most visibly in the form of limited time, limited money, cultural objections to certain practices, and limits to available information. These constraints limit the potential efficacy of household-scale changes as each household is repeating the same small-scale tasks without the possibility of benefiting from economies of scale or a larger transformation of the processes my informants' sustainability practices aim to address. Even if we lived in a world in which my informants had limitless time, money, and information, many of their sustainability practices would prove ineffective because of the limitations built into the society in which my informants find themselves, that is to say, capitalist society. This isn't to say that one should take no responsibility at all, but rather that there are hard limits to the changes that individuals can make on their own.

Suggestions for future research

Social practices research is increasingly gaining recognition by utilities and governments in the United Kingdom and Europe as a useful way to investigate the demand by households for resources like electricity, fuel, and water. However, it is not always clear how to turn the output of this historically situated descriptive research method into policy prescriptions. The approach I have used here, making sense of research on social practices through the use of a conceptual household production function—is potentially a fruitful first step in large-scale quantitative utility or regulatory research that lays the groundwork for policy. There are three areas that I believe could benefit from future investigations using this approach— practices in "conventional" households, in thrift-minded households, and in high-demand households— and a fourth—sustainability work and gender—that would require a more quantitative approach.

Practices in "conventional" households

Throughout this study, I compared the practices of my informants, just as they contrasted themselves, to those of "conventional" households, a nebulous and ill-defined concept at best. Because no social practices investigation of more general household-level demand for resources in the United States has been undertaken, a true comparison of the practices and meanings of practices between my highly eco-conscious informants and the "mainstream" was not possible. This is a potentially fruitful area of future research, particularly when combined with cross-cultural comparative approaches.

Practices in thrift-minded households

The households I spoke with for this study were motivated by ecological considerations to decrease their demand for resources. Other U.S. households may have little to no concern about the environment but may be engaging in practices that allow them to get things done in everyday life while consuming few resources. This may be because of poverty or other reasons, such as a religious belief in simplicity and thrift. Given the nature of climate change opinion in the United States, where only a minority report caring about climate change "a great deal" (Gallup 2016), other reasons that motivate reductions in consumption and their associated practices should be examined. The practices in these households may be instructive, providing new evidence for barriers to change and paths forward.

Practices in high-demand households

While this is a study of households who are taking deliberate steps to decrease their impacts on the environment, social practices research is needed on high-income Americans. Frequent air travel, multiple large homes, and multiple cars are certainly resource-intensive. A better understanding of the social meanings behind these practices from research that takes high-income practitioners and their motivations seriously is needed.

Sustainability work and gender

While my informants expressed to me the view that their heterosexual relationships are egalitarian, the ethnographic methods used here are inadequate for testing the accuracy of these perceptions. There may be unequal divisions of time spent working, whether waged or unwaged, in households. It may be the case that policies and trends that promote sustainability practices create new unwaged work that is primarily socially assigned to women in households. Quantitative time-use research would be needed for this type of analysis.

The futility of household-scale sustainability practices

Changes are needed to mitigate the impacts of climate change, and current large-scale responses such as the Paris Climate Agreement are projected to be inadequate (Schwartz 2016). As this study was undertaken just after the election of Donald Trump, my informants had both increased anxiety about the future of the environment and an increased sense of personal responsibility for environmental preservation.

However, this research has revealed the negative consequences that occur when households take on the work of sustainability in addition to the other goods and services produced by households for their members. The household production of sustainability generates conflicts and it frequently demands additional time, money, and effort from people who may have few resources to spare given all of their other responsibilities. Most poignantly, these household sustainability efforts cause people committed to what Kyle called a "less eco-hostile existence" to make trade-offs, including of their own sanity and parental desires, to get everyday things done in a way that feels consistent with their values. But despite these sacrifices, their efforts frequently fall short of hopes and expectations, such as when they learn after the fact that all of the work they put in to cloth diapering or protecting their children from fluoride was ultimately counterproductive.

Shove et al (2015, 275) argue that because "demand is an outcome of what people do, any radical change depends on reconfiguring the practices that comprise everyday life." However, they also make the point that the extent to which these changes are even possible is limited by existing infrastructures and the complexes of practices that are dependent on them. While Shove and her coauthors are referring to physical infrastructures like buildings and roads, perhaps the economy and society as a whole can also be thought of as infrastructures that likewise constrain possible actions and choices. The logical extension of these theories of social practice is that infrastructures are also dependent on the practices and practitioners that reproduce infrastructures and make them seem necessary and normal. To "reconfigure the practices that comprise everyday life," infrastructures must also be transformed.

Moving forward: pragmatic pathways

Many sustainability-oriented practices take more time or more money than conventional ways of getting things done. They require special equipment that saves resources without changing the meaning of practices and the cultural services involved, such as dual-flush toilets or energy-efficient furnaces. Or, they require large investments in time and self-provisioning to produce substitutes that avoid purchases from the commercial sector, such as "elimination communication" infant toilet training to avoid using diapers altogether or making your own laundry detergent by hand-grating soap. My informants universally reported feeling exhausted by the burden of additional unwaged work in their lives, so paths forward for the environment must avoid increasing these burdens. Three sustainability practices I discussed with my informants offer the intriguing combination of saving both time and money as well as resources: selective flushing, decreasing the frequency of showering, and wearing clothes more times between washes. There is a catch: changing these practices on a wider scale would mean redefining what cleanliness means in the United States, a nation obsessed with being clean.

A major limitation to redefining cleanliness is embedded in the infrastructures used to produce it—cultural expectations and technology are recursively related in ways that reinforce the normalcy of these expectations. Why do toilets flush if we aren't meant to flush them? Why shouldn't I wash my clothes after every wearing when it is easy and convenient to do so? Cross-cultural comparisons of practices offer some reassuring counterevidence, as tumble dryers exist in over half of U.K. households, but 93 percent line-dry their laundry (U.K. Office for National Statistics 2011; Project Laundry List 2013). There isn't a one-to-one relationship between technology and practices—there are historical and cultural forces that impact what we perceive as acceptable ways to get things done.

But the social and cultural meanings of comfort and cleanliness can be changed (Shove et al 2008, 307). Among my informants, a severe drought in California in the late 1980s and early 1990s influenced perceptions of selective flushing, even for informants who had never lived in California (California Department of Water Resources 1993). However, these examples are more the exception than the rule when it comes to the interwoven relationship between institutions, infrastructures, technology, practices, and social meanings. Policies that promote sustainability production within households should, as much as possible, avoid shifting additional work, whether waged or unwaged, onto households, and should instead focus on changing the meanings, infrastructures, and "needs" that motivate practitioners and necessitate practices.

But what would happen if we spent less time engaged in unwaged household production, and what would need to change to make these reductions feasible within capitalism without reducing well-being? In attempting to answer this question for myself, I keep returning to the old Wobbly notion of striking on the job—not a total refusal of unwaged work, but a slowdown. In the United States and many other countries in the Global North, the amount of time spent in housework per household has fallen since the 1960s (Altinas & Sullivan 2016). This trend has possibly involved some outsourcing of previously unwaged household production tasks onto waged workers employed by the household and by substituting purchased inputs like restaurant meals, but it has also undoubtedly involved changing expectations for how clean a house should be and how often household chores should be done. On the other hand, U.S. parents—both mothers and fathers—now spend more time on childcare tasks than they did in the 1960s (Pew Research Center 2013). Would it be so bad if we were all just a little bit dirtier and our children parented a little less intensively? The key, once again, is changing expectations, social meanings, and the definition of "needs."

Moving forward: utopian visions

Just as choices are constrained by the social and economic institutions we find ourselves in, so is our ability to even conceive of possible paths forward outside those institutions. More efficient appliances get the same things done, just using slightly less energy. Similarly, progressive reforms and other adjustments to waged and unwaged work are not sufficient to alleviate the problems faced by my informants: they are exhausted, they feel like they have no time, and they are having to make upsetting trade-offs between their own emotional well-being and their desire for healthy families, communities, and environment.

The obvious culprit in a Marxist-feminist study is capitalist society, pointed to throughout this book as placing limits on the range of possible actions. But simply changing the mode of economic production is not sufficient—the family household must also be transformed. Schor (2011) and Matthaei (2015) have promoted intensive self-provisioning and household production as a pro-environmental alternative to capitalist production and as a liberatory substitute for waged work. However, my interviews with households attempting to make these substitutions reveal that time spent in unwaged work for household production is no less exhausting and depleting than waged work—and in some cases may be even more so. Thus, simply doing away with capitalism is not sufficient if the household and family are not likewise transformed in ways that shorten—or rather abolish—the working day, whether this work is waged or unwaged.

It is nothing new that "even the most radical flare up" at proposals to sublate the family (Marx & Engels 2012 [1848], 88). While notions of collective childrearing in the U.S. mind are often conjured as "a nightmare vision of raising children like Perdue chickens" (Benjamin 1988, 204), this needn't be the case. Despite being idealized and frequently used as a political tool, families are not always healthy and happy and frequently cannot be relied upon as sources of care (Barrett & McIntosh 1982; Quick 2008, 313). Work by Hopkins (2017), Haraway (2016), and Lewis (2019) suggests that postcapitalist paths forward must include transformations not only of the economic system but also of our notions of the household and family. As Marxist-feminists have long pointed out, the contemporary family household was formed by capitalism and at the same time makes possible its continued existence (Vogel 2013 [1983]). Thus, we need to radically redefine what we mean by "kin," the infrastructures and institutions through which we get things done in everyday life, and even what we define as needs.

The household sustainability efforts of my informants, while well intentioned, are most frequently aimed at addressing environmental problems they view as originating at other sites and on other scales. Each household individually repeats common sustainability tasks that could be achieved more effectively collectively or on a larger scale. At the same time, environmental and social problems are caused by the organization of families into individual households, a modern arrangement that is both socially and environmentally taxing. This belief is echoed by my informant, Kyle, when he discusses his reasons for living in intentional community:

Kyle: Everyone doesn't need to have their own washing machine that goes unused 95 percent of the time, or your own car, or your own house! People living in their own houses is just absurd. The consumer culture, driven by the need to sell stuff for ever higher profits, creates these absurdities. And you need to be intentional if you want to do something different.

The households I spoke with over the course of this research are trying their best to, as Kyle suggests, do something different. And some pragmatic reforms that involve changing the social meaning of practices in ways that decrease the demand for resources may provide a practical path forward. But without radical transformations in infrastructures and institutions—including the family household—these efforts will always fall short of what is needed to fully protect people and the environment from harm.

References

Altintas, Evrim and Oriel Sullivan (2016) "Fifty years of change updated: Cross-national gender convergence in housework," *Demographic Research*, 35(2): 455–470.

Andersen, Robin (2013) "The 'Crying Indian,' corporations, and environmentalism: A half-century of struggle over environmental messaging," in Matthew P. McAllister and Emily West (eds) *Routledge Companion to Advertising and Promotional Culture*, New York: Routledge, pp 403–419.

Barrett, Michèle and Mary McIntosh (1982) *The Anti-Social Family*, London: Verso Books.

Benjamin, Jessica (1988) *The Bonds of Love: Psychoanalysis, Feminism and the Problem of Domination*, New York: Pantheon Books.

Bonefeld, Werner (2008) "Global capital, national state, and the international," *Critique*, 36(1): 63–72.

California Department of Water Resources (1993) "California's 1987–92 Drought: A Summary of Six Years of Drought," Available: https://web.archive.org/web/20170628103623/https://water.ca.gov/waterconditions/docs/2_drought-1987-92.pdf [Accessed May 29, 2017].

Collins, Jane L. (1990) "Unwaged labor in comparative perspective: Recent theories and unanswered questions," in Jane L. Collins and Martha Giménez (eds) *Work without Wages: Comparative Studies of Domestic Labor and Self-Employment*, Albany: State University of New York Press, pp 3–24.

Gallup News Service (2016) "Gallup Poll Social Series: Environment," March 6, Available: http://www.gallup.com/file/poll/190055/Global_Warming_Trends_160316%20.pdf [Accessed June 18, 2016].

Hacker, Jacob S. (2006) *The Great Risk Shift: The Assault on American Jobs, Families, Health Care, and Retirement and How You Can Fight Back*, Oxford: Oxford University Press.

Haraway, Donna J. (2016) *Staying with the Trouble*, Durham, NC: Duke University Press.

Hopkins, Barbara E. (2017) "Provisioning under austerity: An evolutionary strategy for meeting human needs through the next millennium," in Richard Westra, Robert Albritton, and Seongjin Jeong (eds) *Varieties of Alternative Economic Systems: Practical Utopias for an Age of Global Crisis and Austerity*, London: Routledge, pp 91–106.

Lewis, Sophie (2019) *Full Surrogacy Now: Feminism against Family*, London: Verso Books.

Marx, Karl and Friedrich Engels (2012 [1848]) *The Communist Manifesto*, edited by Jeffrey C. Isaac, New Haven, CT: Yale University Press.

Matthaei, Julie (2015) "From Inequality to Solidarity: Co-creating a New Economics for the 21st Century," [Unpublished manuscript], August 12, Available: http://www.wellesley.edu/sites/default/files/assets/departme nts/economics/files/matthaei_-from_inequality_to_solidarity-urpe_read er_-_1_12_16.pdf [Accessed August 31, 2022].

Munro, Kirstin (2022) "Overaccumulation, crisis, and the contradictions of household waste sorting," *Capital & Class*, 46(1): 115–131.

Pew Research Center (2013) "Modern Parenthood: Roles of Moms and Dads Converge as They Balance Work and Family," March 14, Available: https://www.pewresearch.org/social-trends/wp-content/uplo ads/sites/3/2013/03/FINAL_modern_parenthood_03-2013.pdf [Accessed August 31, 2022].

Project Laundry List (2013) "Laundry Fact Sheet," Available: http://www. laundrylist.org/wp-content/uploads/2013/08/facts.pdf [Accessed June 22, 2017].

Quick, Paddy (2008) "Unpaid, reproductive, caring labor? The production of labor power? Theoretical and practical implications of terms used for women's work," *Review of Radical Political Economics*, 40(3): 308–314.

Schor, Juliet B. (2011) *True Wealth*, New York: Penguin Books.

Schwartz, Jen (2016) "Why the Paris Climate Agreement Can't Save the Planet," *Popular Science*, February 10, Available: http://www.popsci.com/ paris-climate-agreement [Accessed July 1, 2017].

Shove, Elizabeth, Matt Watson, and Nicola Spurling (2015) "Conceptualizing connections: Energy demand, infrastructures, and social practices," *European Journal of Social Theory*, 18(3): 274–278.

Shove, Elizabeth, Heather Chappells, Loren Lutzenhiser, and Bruce Hackett (2008) "Comfort in a lower carbon society," *Building Research & Information*, 36(4): 307–311.

Strand, Ginger (2008) "The Crying Indian," *Orion Magazine*, November/ December, Available: https://orionmagazine.org/article/the-crying-ind ian/ [Accessed June 25, 2017].

U.K. Office for National Statistics (2011) "Living Costs and Food Survey," Available: http://www.ons.gov.uk/ons/rel/family-spending/family- spending/family-spending-2011-edition/consumer-durables-nugget.xls [Accessed June 22, 2017].

Vogel, Lise (2013 [1983]) *Marxism and the Oppression of Women: Toward a Unitary Theory*, Leiden: Brill.

Notes

Chapter 1

1   While talking about this project with an old friend, she reminded me of a time when, as a teenager who had recently learned about the negative and contradictory aspects of recycling in school, I had thrown an empty beer can in the garbage at the home of some deep green anarcho-primitivist friends in Olympia, Washington, announcing "I don't recycle," for shock value. It was apparently so shocking as to be memorable nearly twenty years later. More recently, I have written critically on the political economy of recycling sorting in Munro (2022).

Chapter 2

1   What I mean by progressive/liberal feminist economics is the branch of democratic socialist economics (see O'Kane & Munro 2022 for a critique of democratic socialist economics) that emerged in the late 1980s and early 1990s as advanced by scholars such as Nancy Folbre (1994), and Marianne Ferber and Julie Nelson (Ferber & Nelson 1993). Progressive/liberal feminist economics aims to overturn male bias in the discipline of economics and argues that women's contributions to the capitalist economy through gendered labor—unpaid or underpaid—are not sufficiently recognized by economists, governments, and society. Feminist economics argues for the recognition of this gendered labor via proposals such as alternative measures of national output that include household production and on the basis of categories such as "care work." In general, it positions itself as an alternative to Marxist-feminism.

2   What I mean by "Social Reproduction Theory" is the work by traditional Marxist scholars such as Arruzza (2016), Bhattacharya (2017), and Ferguson (2019) who have redefined "social reproduction" from its conventional meaning—the reproduction of capitalist society as a whole— to meaning the reproduction of labor-power alone. Social Reproduction Theory argues for the revolutionary capacity and working-class position of unproductive workers whose waged and unwaged work is involved in the reproduction of the commodity labor-power. In my reading, Social Reproduction Theory can be best described as a revolutionary strategy aimed at correctly identifying the working class on the assumption that the correct definition, along with transitional demands (Trotsky 2002 [1938]) connected to the correct identification of the working class, can help to bring about communism.

3   It is reasonable to wonder whether or not spouses interviewed together will provide honest answers to questions about household tasks and who does them. My conversations with four women with male partners (Gloria, Heather, Quinn, and Yvonne), one woman with a female partner (Wendy), and one gender nonbinary informant with a male partner (Leonda) all took place without their partners present for reasons related to scheduling. All of these informants told me, without being prompted to do so, that they believe their

183

relationships and households are egalitarian, though Leonda did have some complaints about their messy male roommate. Of the informants in heterosexual relationships, four of the 14 women (Gloria, Mina, Vanessa, and Yvonne) described themselves as stay-at-home mothers at the time of the interview, though Yvonne is an urban homesteader who also contributes substantial time to her husband's permaculture business. Ian, a self-employed artist, was the primary parent tasked with childcare and other household production responsibilities while his partner Ivy is the primary breadwinner and works outside the home. A number of my informants had chosen extended breastfeeding reaching into the toddler years, and this is a time-consuming practice that can't easily be shared by non-birth partners. However, it was difficult to discern any other major imbalances in the overall amount of time spent in work (whether waged or unwaged).

4   Reid (1934) notes that not all goods and services produced by the household are necessarily "good" for individual household members or the household as a whole. Some examples include gay conversion therapy, smoking and drug use, alcohol and unhealthy food, dangerous hoarding and other compulsive behaviors, and forms of entertainment that annoy or even harm other household members.

5   Which, of course, is not to say that advertising plays no role at all—recall the scene from 2006 film *The Devil Wears Prada* when magazine editor Miranda points out to Andy, "it's sort of comical that you think you've made a choice ... In fact, you are wearing a sweater that was selected for you by the people in this room."

Index

References to notes show both the page number and the note number (231n3).

Printed and bound by CPI Group (UK) Ltd, Croydon, CR0 4YY

23/04/2025

14661025-0001